101 MOVIES

TO SEE BEFORE YOU GROW UP

BE YOUR OWN MOVIE CRITIC—
THE MUST-SEE MOVIE LIST FOR KIDS

Walter Foster
Jr.

Movies are made to entertain! A movie can make you think, teach you a lesson about life, introduce you to fascinating make-believe friends, or let you explore an exciting fantasy world for a few hours. This book is filled with 101 of the most popular movies for families, children, and movie-lovers of all ages. Use it as your own personal movie handbook—learn cool trivia and interesting details to look for as you watch each film, and then check the movie off your list after you've seen it. Each film has its own page and features basic information, such as the director, rating, release date, awards, and other quick facts you can use to impress your friends. From classic films to modern flicks, including animated, adventure, action, sports, and musical genres, you'll find plenty of films to create your own movie bucket list. Grab some popcorn and find a comfy place to curl up—the show is about to begin!

Quarto is the authority on a wide range of topics.
Quarto educates, entertains and enriches the lives of our readers—enthusiasts and lovers of hands-on living.
www.quartoknows.com

Cover design by: Steve Scott
Written by: Suzette Valle
Illustrated by: Natasha Hellegourach

6 Orchard Road, Suite 100
Lake Forest, CA 92630
quartoknows.com
Visit our blogs @quartoknows.com

Printed in China
1 3 5 7 9 10 8 6 4 2

IOI MOVIES
TO SEE BEFORE YOU GROW UP

Be sure to check the rating of each film, and ask your parents about movies rated "PG" or "PG-13," mate.

Use the bottom of the page to mark off each movie after you watch it!

Look for the symbol at the top of each page to see how many Academy Awards the movie has won.

WRITTEN BY SUZETTE VALLE
ILLUSTRATED BY NATASHA HELLEGOURACH

TABLE OF CONTENTS

The movies in this book are divided by film genre and listed in random order, so you can start watching wherever you like. We think it's practically perfect in every way!

1

IT'S A WONDERFUL LIFE

DIRECTOR:
Frank Capra

RELEASE DATE:
January 7, 1947

RATED:
NR
Not Rated

RUNTIME:
2 hours,
10 minutes

THE STORY

George Bailey (James Stewart) would rather die than live another miserable day. Clarence (Henry Travers), a guardian angel, is sent to Earth to save Bailey, but before he swoops in, he is shown flashbacks of George's life. At age 12, George lost hearing in one ear after rescuing his younger brother from a frozen pond. At 21, George's father unexpectedly died, and George unselfishly took over the family business, Bailey Building and Loan Association. Things go terribly wrong with the business after a large deposit is lost. George and his wife, Mary (Donna Reed), sacrifice their honeymoon money to help the business, but the bank still fails to thrive. Facing fraud and jail, George decides he's worth more dead than alive. He's about to jump off a bridge when Clarence is dispatched from heaven to save him. The angel shows George what his family and town would have been like without him, and he's shocked by what he sees. Seeing his life from a whole new perspective, George begs his guardian angel to let him live: "I want to live, Clarence!"

What does this famous Christmas film teach us? George Bailey already had a wonderful life, and he didn't even know it!

STARRING:
James Stewart, Donna Reed, and Lionel Barrymore

MUSIC:
Songs by Dimitri Tiomkin

SCREEN-PLAY WRITTEN BY:
Philip Van Doren Stern

DID YOU KNOW?

In 1939, Philip Van Doren Stern wrote "The Greatest Gift," which became *It's a Wonderful Life.* After he failed to find a publisher, he made 200 copies of the tale and sent them as Christmas cards in 1943.

Saw it! ☐ Rating: ☆☆☆☆☆

Date: ___ / ___ / _____ With: _____

Notes: _____

_____

2

HOME ALONE

DIRECTOR:
Chris
Columbus

RELEASE DATE:
November 16, 1990

RATED:
PG
for comic action
and mild language

RUNTIME:
1 hour,
43 minutes

THE STORY

Kevin McCallister (Macaulay Caulkin) is a cheeky and resourceful 8-year-old boy. As the youngest and smallest member of his family, he's tired of being picked on and ignored. Kevin secretly wishes that his family would disappear. The night before the big family Christmas trip to Europe, a power outage resets the alarm clocks. Everyone wakes up late the next morning and scrambles to get to the airport on time. In the chaos, Kevin is left behind! He wakes up to an empty house, and at first, he's thrilled! However, his joy is short-lived when he finds out two thieves, Harry (Joe Pesci) and Marv (Daniel Stern), are roaming the neighborhood planning to break in. Meanwhile, Kate McCallister (Catherine O'Hara), Kevin's mom, is frantically trying to get back to Chicago from Paris, but all of the flights are full. To protect his home from the bandits, Kevin rigs the house with booby traps. Will Mrs. McCallister and the rest of the family get home in time to save Kevin? Or is it really the bandits who need the saving from Kevin's elaborate contraptions?

WATCH OUT FOR

The success of *Home Alone* led to multiple films, *Home Alone 2: Lost in New York* (1992) and *Home Alone 3* (1997), and TV movies, *Home Alone 4* (2002) and *Home Alone: The Holiday Heist* (2012).

DID YOU KNOW?

Home Alone had a $15 million budget and grossed $477 million worldwide. *Home Alone* was entered into the Guinness Book of World Records as the "Highest Grossing Live Action Comedy" of 1990.

Saw it! ☐ Rating: ☆☆☆☆☆

Date: ___/___/_____ With: _____

Notes: _____

_____

🎭🎭🎭 3 ACADEMY AWARDS

MIRACLE ON 34TH STREET

THE STORY

Kris Kringle (Edmund Gwenn) is inspecting the Macy's Thanksgiving Day parade lineup when he notices that the man hired by parade organizer Doris Walker (Maureen O'Hara) to play Santa Claus shows up drunk. Kringle turns up just in time, and Doris hires him on the spot. Kringle is a natural as Santa—beard, belly, and all—so Doris hires him to work as the store's Santa Claus as well. But when the jolly man recommends that customers buy from rival stores when they have better prices, Doris gets mad at first. But the customers love him, and they love Macy's for its kind heart!

However, Kris is so realistic as Santa that many of the children start believing he's the real thing! The store executives begin to get annoyed with Kris's persistence that he is the real Santa Claus, and they want to have his mental health evaluated by a judge. Fred Gailey (John Payne) is a lawyer and also a friend of Doris and her young daughter, Susan (Natalie Wood). At Kris's court hearing, Fred proves Kris Kringle is the real Santa Claus! On Christmas morning, Kris sends Fred, Doris, and Susan home through a shortcut. On the way, they see Doris's dream house with a "For Sale" sign, and they stop to see it. What they find inside makes them all firm believers.

DID YOU KNOW?

Before the first helium balloon (Felix the Cat) debuted at the Macy's Thanksgiving Day Parade in 1927, live 200 animals used to march along the six-mile route!

DIRECTOR:
George Seaton

RELEASE DATE:
May 2, 1947

RATED:
NR
Not Rated

RUNTIME:
1 hour,
36 minutes

Saw it! ☐ Rating: ☆☆☆☆☆

Date: ___/___/_____ With: _____

Notes: _____

_____

4

THE PARENT TRAP

RELEASE DATE:
June 21, 1961

RATED:

G

General Audiences

RUNTIME:
2 hours,
9 minutes

Can you imagine having to act the part of two different people with different accents? In the 1961 Disney film, *The Parent Trap,* Hayley Mills plays the role of identical twin girls, one from Boston and the other from California.

THE STORY

Separated at birth when their parents divorced, Susan and Sharon each grew up living with one parent, unaware of the other twin's existence. Sharon

lives in Boston with her mother, while Susan lives with her father in California. They bump into each other for the first time at summer camp, and their first encounter is awkward! After some initial rivalry leads to campground mischief, the two become friends and realize they are sisters. Together they scheme to switch places to get to know the opposite parent—and get rid of their father's fiancée to reunite their parents.

In Disney's 1998 remake, Lindsay Lohan marvelously plays the role of the twins. One girl lives in London with her mother, a famous wedding gown designer, and the other lives in California with her dad. Hallie and Annie fabricate elaborate shenanigans to get their parents to reconcile and arrive at the expected happy ending.

WATCH OUT FOR

What makes *The Parent Trap* so interesting is that one actress plays two parts, which was an amazing feat for the filmmakers to achieve. Have a movie marathon with both films, and see how many differences you notice as you watch the same plot unfold twice, three decades apart!

DID YOU KNOW?

Hayley Mills had to learn American slang since she's British. Lindsay Lohan was only 11 years old when she starred in *The Parent Trap* remake, and she learned to speak with a British accent!

STARRING:
Hayley Mills, Maureen O'Hara, and Brian Keith

MUSIC:
Songs by Richard M. Sherman and Robert B. Sherman

SPECIAL FX:
Double exposure scenes using one actress to play twins

Saw it! ☐ Rating: ☆☆☆☆☆

Date: ___/___/_____ With: _____

Notes: _____

_____

5

3 ACADEMY AWARDS

TO KILL A MOCKINGBIRD

DIRECTOR:
Robert Mulligan

RELEASE DATE:
March 16, 1963

RATED:

NR

Not Rated

RUNTIME:
2 hours,
9 minutes

WHY IT'S FAMOUS

This film's screenplay, based on the 1960 Pulitzer Prize-winning novel of the same name by Harper Lee, illustrates the profound racial problems and injustices of the 1930s in the Deep South.

THE STORY

Atticus Finch (Gregory Peck) is an honest, well-respected attorney and a widower. He is raising his two children, 6-year-old Scout (Mary Badham), and 10-year-old Jeremy "Jem" (Phillip Alford), on his own. Scout narrates the story about her family living in the fictional town of Maycomb, Alabama. The kids preoccupy themselves by spying on their strange neighbor, Arthur "Boo" Radley (Robert Duvall), who seems to never leave his house. Meanwhile, Mr. Finch is appointed to defend a black man, Tom Robinson (Brock Peters), who is accused of raping a white woman. The Finch family faces scorn from the townspeople, who believe the man is guilty of the crime even before he's tried. Atticus uses the situation to teach his children about prejudice and intolerance. Unexpectedly, the children are attacked by a bigoted, resentful citizen, but they're saved by an unlikely friend.

DID YOU KNOW?

Mary Badham was 10 years old when she played the role of Scout. She had never acted before, and was nominated for an Oscar for Best Supporting Actress.

Saw it! ☐ Rating: ☆☆☆☆☆
Date: ___ / ___ / _____ With: _____
Notes: _____
_____

HOLES

THE STORY

At Camp Green Lake, a juvenile correction center located in the middle of the desert, there's no lake—only dirt and holes as far as the eye can see. The Warden, Louise Walker (Sigourney Weaver), and Mr. Sir (Jon Voight), the head counselor, are mean-spirited and make sure the boys at the camp stick to their punishment; each boy has to dig one hole a day, and every hole must be 5 feet deep and 5 feet wide. Stanley Yelnats IV (Shia LaBeouf) is from a nice family and was sent to Camp Green for stealing a pair of sneakers worn and donated by a famous ball player. If the boys dig up something interesting, such as a fossil, they earn a day off from digging under the hot sun. Stanley uncovers a lipstick tube with the initials K.B. engraved on it, but gives it to another boy who hasn't had a day off in six months! One day, Stanley ends up at the Warden's home. He notices old newspapers and wanted posters for Kissing Kate Barlow (Patricia Arquette), and they remind him of the initials on the lipstick tube. Zero (Khleo Thomas) and Stanley become friends, and they try to run away from camp together but face dangerous obstacles. Stories within stories start to unfold, which help us understand the lipstick and our young heroes' fate.

DID YOU KNOW?

Stanley Yelnats' last name is a palindrome—written backwards, it spells his first name.

DIRECTOR:
Andrew Davis

RELEASE DATE:
April 18, 2003

RATED:
PG
for violence, mild language, and some thematic elements

RUNTIME:
1 hour, 57 minutes

Saw it! ☐   Rating: ☆☆☆☆☆
Date: ___/___/_____ With: _____
Notes: _____
_____

HOMEWARD BOUND: THE INCREDIBLE JOURNEY

DIRECTOR:
Duwayne Dunham

RELEASE DATE:
February 12, 1993

RATED:
G
General Audiences

RUNTIME:
1 hour, 24 minutes

THE STORY

Three pets are left with a friend at a ranch while their owners go on a trip. But Chance (Michael J. Fox), an American Bulldog puppy; Shadow (Don Ameche), an older Golden Retriever; and Sassy (Sally Field), a mischievous Himalayan cat, think they've been abandoned. They bravely escape from the ranch in search of their home and family. Their journey takes them over the breathtaking California Sierra Mountains, rivers, and forests. These wisecracking pals will crack you up throughout their rough adventure. Bears, mountain lions, and even the ferocity of Mother Nature won't keep these animals from their family!

WATCH OUT FOR

The animal stunts the trainers pulled off in this film are amazing. In one scene, a dog lures a mountain lion onto the end of a log, while another dog jumps on the other end to hurl the wildcat into the river!

DID YOU KNOW?

4 Golden Retrievers, 4 American Bulldogs, and 8 Himalayan cats were trained over 7 months to play the parts of Shadow, Chance, and Sassy.

UP NEXT

The adventures continue in *Homeward Bound II: Lost in San Francisco* (1996). The trio of pets once again find themselves trying to find their way home—this time in a big city!

Saw it! ☐ Rating: ☆☆☆☆☆
Date: ___ / ___ / _____ With: _____
Notes: _____
_____

THE BRAVE LITTLE TOASTER

The Brave Little Toaster, common household appliances with simple names such as Toaster, Radio, Lampy, Blanky, and Kirby come to life. They go through harrowing adventures—but they prevail in the end. Hooray! Who doesn't like a happy ending, right? Well, it's not quite that simple. As in real life, a little struggle makes the happy ending that much sweeter.

DIRECTOR:
Jerry Rees

THE STORY

These ordinary household appliances sit in Rob's summer cabin waiting for him to visit. As time goes by and their owner doesn't come back, they start to feel abandoned. But they refuse to accept the idea that their owner doesn't want them anymore. Toaster, the leader of the pack, tells the domestic devices that they must find Rob to once again feel loved. Convinced by Toaster, they set out to find their master. Along the way, the appliances learn the values of teamwork, bravery, friendship, and perseverance.

RELEASE DATE:
July 10, 1987
(USA)

RATED:
NR
with mild scary scenes

WHY IT'S FAMOUS

When John Lasseter was a junior animator at Disney, *The Brave Little Toaster* was his first attempt to make a computer-generated imagery (CGI) film. Though Disney rejected the idea, Lasseter went on to change the future of animation with the CGI concept and later became the chief creative officer for Walt Disney Animation and Pixar!

RUNTIME:
1 hour,
30 minutes

Saw it! ☐ Rating: ☆☆☆☆☆
Date: ___/___/_____ With: _____
Notes: _____
_____

9

BABE

DIRECTOR:
Chris Noonan

RELEASE DATE:
August 4, 1995

RATED:

G

General Audiences

RUNTIME:
1 hour, 29 minutes

THE STORY

A little pig wants to be a sheepherder to save himself from certain death. Babe, an orphaned piglet whose mother was slaughtered, knows it's the only way he will survive living on Mr. Hoggett's farm. Babe went home with Mr. Hoggett as a prize from a county fair; however, Babe can't escape being eyed as the next centerpiece for Christmas dinner. Babe learns that humans eat pigs, so he decides to run away. When Hoggett finally finds him, he feeds him and sings to comfort him. Attempting to make himself useful around the farm, Babe tries to herd the farmer's sheep by speaking to them. When Mr. Hoggett sees Babe's talent, he enters him into a sheepherding competition that ends with the farmer acknowledging Babe's efforts by saying, "That'll do pig. That'll do."

WHY IT'S FAMOUS

Babe was nominated for several Academy Awards, winning for Best Visual Effects. It was also commended for raising awareness about animal abuse. During its time, *Babe* influenced many young people to rethink the food they were eating; and based on interactions between the animals in the film, many concluded that animals are capable of feeling sadness, happiness, and pain.

DID YOU KNOW?

The American Film Institute named *Babe* one of the most inspiring films of all time. According to *AFI's 100 Years of Cheers*, *Babe* "sends us from the theater with a greater sense of possibility and hope for the future."

Saw it! ☐ Rating: ☆☆☆☆☆

Date: ___/___/_____ With: _____

Notes: _____

_____

4 ACADEMY AWARDS

E.T. THE EXTRA-TERRESTRIAL

THE STORY

Elliot (Henry Thomas) is 10 years old when he finds a little goblin-like alien stranded in his backyard. Elliot, his older brother Michael (Robert McNaughton), and his little sister Gertie (Drew Barrymore), hide E.T. in their house. Elliot notices that E.T. copies his gestures, and he eventually begins to feel a strange connection with the alien. One day, the kids leave E.T. at home while they go to school, and the curious alien explores around the house. After looking through a comic book, E.T. gets the idea to build a device to call home. Elliot helps him make a contraption out of an electronic toy, a tin can, and miscellaneous metal parts. Soon the extraterrestrial's health starts to weaken, and Elliot also begins to get sick. Government agents show up at Elliot's house and isolate both him and E.T. Suddenly, Elliot and E.T. regain their strength, and with his brother's help, they escape authorities by flying into the night sky on a bicycle. Does E.T. make it home? Watch *E.T.* and find out!

DID YOU KNOW?

Elliot's parents are divorced in the film. When Steven Spielberg's parents were going through a divorce, the director made up imaginary friends who would help him temporarily escape his sadness.

DIRECTOR:
Steven Spielberg

RELEASE DATE:
June 11, 1982

RATED:

PG

for language and mild thematic elements

WHY IT'S FAMOUS

E.T. presents a remarkable portrait of childhood innocence, along with the heartwarming friendship between a boy and an alien. This classic piece of movie magic lives on as an ideal film for the whole family.

RUNTIME:
1 hour, 55 minutes

Saw it! ☐ Rating: ☆☆☆☆☆
Date: ___ / ___ / _____ With: _____
Notes: _____
_____

11

TOY STORY

DIRECTOR:
John Lasseter

RELEASE DATE:
November 22, 1995

RATED:

G

General Audiences

RUNTIME:
1 hour,
21 minutes

THE STORY

Classic toys (a cowboy named Woody and a space ranger named Buzz) come to life when their owner, a boy named Andy, is not around. Andy's family is moving, so he has an early birthday party. The adventure begins when Andy's mom tells him he can take only one toy to Pizza Planet for dinner. A jealous Woody (Tom Hanks) tries to hide Buzz (Tim Allen), who is convinced he's a real space ranger, so Andy will take him instead. In the heat of the moment, Woody accidentally pushes Buzz out of the bedroom window. Because he can't find Buzz, Andy reluctantly takes Woody—but Buzz manages to climb into the

car as it pulls out of the driveway. At the restaurant, Buzz jumps inside an arcade game that looks like a spaceship, and Woody follows, trying to convince Buzz to find Andy so the two can go home. Sid, Andy's toy-destroying next door neighbor, pulls Woody and Buzz from the machine and takes them home. Woody and Buzz learn they must work together to escape Sid and get back to Andy's house before he moves away!

UP NEXT
Toy Story was followed by *Toy Story 2* (1999) and *Toy Story 3* (2010). *Toy Story 4* is set to release in 2017.

WHY IT'S FAMOUS
Toy Story is the first full-length film to use computer-generated imagery (CGI). Its development and pioneering of CGI techniques made this first full-length computer-animated film a standout achievement in the film industry.

STARRING:
Tom Hanks
and
Tim Allen

MUSIC:
Songs by
Randy
Newman

DID YOU KNOW?
Woody and Buzz Lightyear were brought to life by John Lasseter at Pixar Animation Studios. Lasseter worked at George Lucas's Industrial Light & Magic until Apple cofounder Steve Jobs bought the graphics group in 1986 and named the studio Pixar. *Toy Story* was a joint project between Pixar and Disney. After the success of *Finding Nemo, The Incredibles,* and other films, Disney purchased Pixar in 2006 for a whopping $7.4 billion.

SPECIAL FX:
First feature film to use computer-generated imagery (CG1) animation

Saw it! ☐ Rating: ☆☆☆☆☆
Date: ___/___/_____ With: _____
Notes: _____
_____

12

FANTASTIC MR. FOX

DIRECTOR:
Wes Anderson

RELEASE DATE:
November 25, 2009

RATED:
PG
for adult content, mild violence

RUNTIME:
1 hour,
27 minutes

THE STORY

The Fox family is entirely proper. Mr. Fox (George Clooney) wears pants, a button-down shirt, and a tie. Felicity Fox (Meryl Streep) wears an apron in the kitchen to make sure her dress doesn't get dirty. Ash (Jason Schwartzman), their broody son, prefers to wear a cape and his pants tucked into his socks. Odd? No. He's just...different! The Fox family has decided to live a less risky life: Instead of stealing chickens and being chased by farmers, Mr. Fox does the next logical thing—he becomes a journalist!

But deep down, a fox will always be a fox. Mr. Fox goes behind Mrs. Fox's back and sneakily gets back into the chicken-nabbing business. Because he has to dig tunnels to capture his prey, he secretly gets help from his friends. But the angry farmers are on to them! The three neighboring farmers, Walter Boggis, Nathan Bunce, and Franklin Bean, stake out the fox's home, waiting for him to come up for food. Can the clever Mr. Fox outfox the farmers?

UP NEXT

Fantastic Mr. Fox is based on the children's book by Roald Dahl. Where have you heard this name before? He also wrote *Charlie and the Chocolate Factory*, *James and the Giant Peach*, and *Matilda*.

Saw it! ☐ Rating: ☆☆☆☆☆

Date: ___/___/_____ With: _____

Notes: _____

_____

CHICKEN RUN

"Claymation," or clay animation, is the art of making clay figures come to life on screen with movement and voice. *Chicken Run* uses this technique to create the barracks-style coop life inhabited by two feisty fowl and their fellow chickens.

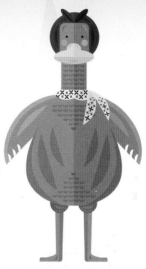

THE STORY

Mr. and Mrs. Tweedy run a chicken coop in England. They sell the chickens' eggs to make a living; however, the chickens are not happy with their living arrangement and want to escape! Ginger (Julia Sawalha), the leader of the group, can't stop thinking of ways to escape, but she fails each time they try to fly the coop. Why? Because chickens can't fly! But Ginger doesn't believe it. When a self-absorbed American rooster, Rocky (Mel Gibson), accidentally flies into the coop, Ginger thinks he can teach the hens to fly too. The urge to escape reaches a frantic peak when the hens find out the egg business isn't doing well, and that Mr. Tweedy (Tony Haygarth) is going to start selling chicken pot pies instead.

WATCH OUT FOR

The combination of the hens' proper British accents and the voice of Mel Gibson as Rocky, the big-headed American rooster, makes for a funny clash of cultures and an engaging film. *Chicken Run* is from the creators of the Wallace and Gromit short films and is their first feature-length, stop motion, claymation movie.

DIRECTORS:
Peter Lord and
Nick Park

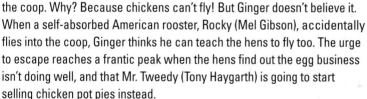

RELEASE DATE:
June 23, 2000

RATED:
G
General
Audiences

RUNTIME:
1 hour,
24 minutes

Saw it! ☐ Rating: ☆☆☆☆☆

Date: ___/___/_____ With: _____

Notes: _____

_____

14

MONSTERS, INC.

DIRECTOR:
Pete Docter

RELEASE DATE:
November 2, 2001

RATED:
G
General Audiences

RUNTIME:
1 hour, 32 minutes

THE STORY

Children's screams power the city of Monstropolis, a parallel world where friendly monsters roam the streets. Sulley Sullivan (John Goodman) and Mike Wazowski (Billy Crystal) are "scarers" who work for Monsters, Inc., the power company responsible for collecting electricity-producing screams. However, the monsters of Monstropolis are terrified of children because they think human children are contaminated and dangerous to touch!

After work one night, a little girl walks through her closet door onto the scarefloor—and bumps right into Sulley! Chaos erupts when Boo, as Sulley nicknames her, escapes into Monstropolis. Boo thinks Sulley and Mike are really funny, and when she giggles, she creates a power surge! The villain, Randall (Steve Buscemi), wants to trap Boo and use her screams to power the city. Can Sulley and Mike save Boo and send her home?

UP NEXT

The CGI (computer-generated imagery) animated *Monsters, Inc.* has a prequel, *Monsters University* (2013). In this film, we find out how Mike and Sully met and became friends in college.

DID YOU KNOW?

After 16 nominations, Randy Newman finally won an Academy Award for Best Original Song in 2002 for "If I Didn't Have You," featured in *Monsters, Inc.*

Saw it! ☐ Rating: ☆☆☆☆☆
Date: ___/___/_____ With: _____
Notes: _____
_____

 **1 ACADEMY AWARD**

FINDING NEMO

Hop aboard the East Australian Current (EAC), dude! Join Dory, Marlin, and their sea turtle friends in an exciting quest to find Marlin's son, Nemo.

DIRECTORS:
Andrew Stanton and Lee Unkrich

THE STORY

Nemo and Marlin (Albert Brooks) live near the Great Barrier Reef. Nemo (Alexander Gould) has an unusually small fin, and after losing his mother when he was just an egg, his dad constantly worries about him. On his first day of school, Nemo gets kidnapped by a scuba diver! The scuba diver, a dentist from Sydney, puts Nemo in a fish tank in his office, and he plans to give Nemo to his mischievous niece, Darla (LuLu Ebeling), as a birthday gift. Marlin searches for his son across the ocean as he travels toward Sydney. Along the way, Marlin meets Dory (Ellen DeGeneres), a royal blue tang fish with short-term memory loss. Together they "just keep swimming," and with the help of a few unexpected friends, Marlin and Dory work together to rescue Nemo and bring him home!

DID YOU KNOW?
John Lasseter, the head of Pixar, assigned crew members who worked on *Finding Nemo* to get scuba-diving certifications.

RELEASE DATE:
May 30, 2003

RATED:

G

General Audiences

WHY IT'S FAMOUS

Finding Nemo showcases Pixar's vivid, flawless CGI (computer-generated imagery) animation. To create this undersea world, crew members traveled to the Great Barrier Reef in Australia to see the natural wonder firsthand. *Finding Dory*, the sequel, followed in June 2016.

RUNTIME:
1 hour, 40 minutes

Saw it! ☐ Rating: ☆☆☆☆☆☆

Date: ___/___/_____ With: _____

Notes: _____

_____

1 ACADEMY AWARD

16 RATATOUILLE

DIRECTOR:
Brad Bird and
Jan Pinkava

RELEASE DATE:
June 29, 2007

RATED:
G
General
Audiences

RUNTIME:
1 hour,
51 minutes

THE STORY

Remy (Patton Oswalt) is a rat with a gift for smell and an exquisite taste in food. After his family is forced to leave their home, he finds himself lost in Paris. Resting on a skylight above Gusteau's, a famous French restaurant started by chef Auguste Gusteau (Brad Garrett), he watches as Linguini, the clumsy garbage boy, accidentally spills a pot of soup. Linguini (Lou Romano) tries to make another pot, but it tastes awful! Remy can't resist, and he secretly fixes the soup. Linguini sees Remy adding spices to the soup, but before he can say anything, the restaurant's new owner chases the rat out of the kitchen. In the scuffle, the soup is mistakenly served and the customers love it! Colette (Janeane Garofalo), the female chef, thinks it was Linguini who made the soup and hires him as a cook. With Remy's clever (and secret) help, Linguini learns to cook and the restaurant gains popularity. Anton Ego (Peter O'Toole), a famous food critic, decides to visit the restaurant. The night of the review, Remy is hurt because Linguini takes Colette's cooking advice over his own. After they argue, Remy brings his rat family to infest the pantry and steal food. Linguini catches Remy red-handed, but he realizes he owes his success to Remy and has treated him badly. He apologizes and tells the staff about his rat sidekick—and they all leave! But the restaurant still has to impress Ego and get a good review. What will they do?

DID YOU KNOW?

The ratatouille recipe used in this movie was created by Chef Thomas Keller for his famous restaurant, French Laundry, in Napa Valley, California.

Saw it! ☐ Rating: ☆☆☆☆☆
Date: ___/___/_____ With: _____
Notes: _____
_____

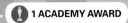 **1 ACADEMY AWARD**

WALL-E

THE STORY

As one of the last robots left on earth, WALL-E's job is to collect the garbage, compress it into perfect cubes, and stack them on top of each other, building enormous skyscrapers. WALL-E (Ben Burtt) carries a small cooler with him to collect any special objects he finds. Each night, WALL-E empties the cooler and reviews the day's treasures; a spork, an iPod, a Rubik's Cube, and a green plant he keeps in an old shoe. He then takes off his tread wheels and powers down for the night. One day, his routine is forever changed by the arrival of a mysterious spaceship. EVE (Elissa Knight), a modern and powerful scouting robot, flies out of the ship and captures WALL-E's attention. They communicate in a stream of distinct whirls and purring sounds. WALL-E falls in love with EVE and doesn't feel lonely anymore. But when EVE finds WALL-E's plant, she grabs it, stores it inside her compartment, and deactivates. WALL-E doesn't understand that EVE was sent to find any signs of life left on Earth. The spaceship arrives to pick up EVE, and WALL-E hitches a ride to *Axiom*, the mother ship, to try to protect his friend. When they arrive, WALL-E and EVE discover that the fate of mankind rests in their hands.

DID YOU KNOW?

EVE stands for "Extraterrestrial Vegetation Evaluator." WALL-E means "Waste Allocation Load Lifter, Earth Class."

DIRECTOR:
Andrew Stanton

RELEASE DATE:
June 27, 2008

RATED:

G

General Audiences

RUNTIME:
1 hour, 37 minutes

Saw it! ☐ Rating: ☆☆☆☆☆

Date: ___/___/_____ With: _____

Notes: _____

_____

18

THE IRON GIANT

DIRECTOR:
Brad Bird

RELEASE DATE:
August 6, 1999

RATED:
PG
for fantasy action
and mild language

RUNTIME:
1 hour,
26 minutes

This animated movie takes place in 1957 during the Cold War when the Soviet Union was America's worst enemy. During the same year, the Russians launched Sputnik, the first satellite to orbit the earth.

THE STORY

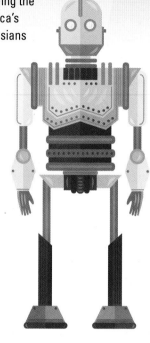

Near Maine, people gazing at Sputnik as it moves across the sky don't notice the Iron Giant (Vin Diesel) crash into the ocean. He stomps his way through the forest eating small metal sources like TV antennas until he stumbles on a power plant. Hogarth Hughes (Eli Marienthal), a 9-year-old boy, lives with his mom (Jennifer Aniston), and notices their TV antenna is suddenly missing. He sees a trail outside and decides to investigate. It leads him to the power plant, where he finds the giant tangled in the high voltage wires he wants to eat! Hogarth shuts off the electricity and saves the giant. Then he hides the Iron Giant in his barn and reads comic books to him. Giant likes Superman's hero qualities, but he learns that superpowers can be used for evil as well. Hogarth tells him, "You are who you choose to be." Meanwhile, the military is looking for the source of the town's destruction and finds evidence leading to Hogarth. Hogarth, his mom, and an artist (Harry Connick Jr.) disguise the seemingly indestructible giant—but can they save him?

Saw it! ☐ Rating: ☆☆☆☆☆

Date: ___/___/_____ With: _____

Notes: _____

_____

JAMES AND THE GIANT PEACH

This film includes a mix of live action and stop motion animation. The director chose this combination to reinforce the transition from reality to fantasy.

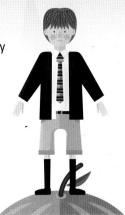

THE STORY

James (Paul Terry) lives happily with his mom and dad in England. The family dreams of visiting New York City. When James's parents are killed, things abruptly change—he's sent to live with his horrible aunts, Spiker and Sponge, who mistreat him. Sad and lonely, James meets an old man with a bag full of crocodile tongues. The stranger gives James the bag and tells him the tongues are magical and that they'll make his life better. But he can't let them get loose! James turns around and promptly trips, spilling the tongues on the ground. That night, right in that very spot, a giant peach starts to grow, and it becomes as big as his house! One day, James takes a bite out of the peach and discovers a tunnel into the fruit. He climbs through and finds amazingly oversized bugs: Old Green Grasshopper (Simon Callow), Centipede (Richard Dreyfuss), Spider (Susan Sarandon), Earthworm (David Thewlis), and Ladybug (Jane Leeves). Together they take a trip to New York aboard the giant peach!

DID YOU KNOW?

Roald Dahl refused to let anyone make a movie about his book *James and the Giant Peach* while he was alive. However, after his death in 1990, his wife Felicity Dahl sold the film rights to Walt Disney.

DIRECTOR:
Henry Selick

RELEASE DATE:
April 12, 1996

RATED:
PG
for some frightening images

RUNTIME:
1 hour, 19 minutes

Saw it! ☐ Rating: ☆☆☆☆☆
Date: ___/___/_____ With: _____
Notes: _____
_____

20 BRAVE

DIRECTORS:
Mark Andrews and Brenda Chapman

RELEASE DATE:
June 22, 2012

RATED:
PG
for some scary action and rude humor

RUNTIME:
1 hour, 39 minutes

THE STORY

Brave is a computer-animated fantasy film about a feisty Scottish princess battling traditions to make her own path. Merida (Kelly Macdonald) doesn't want to marry one of the three suitors chosen from the neighboring clans. Queen Elinor (Emma Thompson) pleads with her stubborn daughter to allow one of the young men to marry her—if she refuses, the Dunbroch clan could face war with the other clans. Like many young girls, Merida takes her anger out on her mother. The fiery redhead follows the will-o'-the-wisps, tiny spirit-like fairies, into the forest. There, Merida meets a sorceress who gives her a bewitched cake that turns her mom into a bear! The witch tells Merida that unless the bond between her and her mother is restored by the second sunrise, Queen Elinor will remain a black bear forever. Merida regrets her behavior and is desperate to find a way to reverse the curse. In the meantime, the clans are already waging war against each other. Can the actions of a single girl change the kingdom's long-standing traditions and allow a princess to marry who and when she wants?

DID YOU KNOW?
Terms like "bunch of galoots" (many fools) and "jiggery pokery" (nonsense) used in the film are real Scottish words and phrases.

Saw it! ☐ Rating: ☆☆☆☆☆

Date: ___/___/_____ With: _____

Notes: _____

_____

A BUG'S LIFE

Have you ever wondered what happens when ants disappear through the tiny pinhole on top of an anthill? We get an up-close, bug's eye view of life underground in this computer-animated movie!

THE STORY

In a moment of panic, an ant screams, "I'm lost! Where's the line?" A leaf has fallen on the trail and blocked the path. The rescue ants come over and say, "Now, stay calm. We are going around the leaf!" The ants are in a hurry to gather enough food for the winter, not only for the colony, but also for a troop of demanding grasshoppers that have made the ants their slaves. Flik (Dave Foley) is a clever ant in the colony who always thinking outside the box. He is tired of Hopper (Kevin Spacey), the leader of the grasshoppers, threatening the colony and stealing their food. However, the Queen (Phyllis Diller), Princess Atta (Julia Louis-Dreyfus), and Mr. Soil (Roddy McDowall) want Flik to stop causing trouble. They encourage Flik to leave the colony to find a band of soldiers that can help protect the colony from the grasshoppers. Flik brings back a silly-looking group of performers from P.T. Flea's Circus. Can they save the colony from the terrifying Hopper?

DID YOU KNOW?

The film crew put Lego wheels on a tiny camera and mounted it on a stick. They rolled it through the garden at Pixar Animation's studio to see what the bugs actually saw!

DIRECTORS:
John Lasseter
and
Andrew Stanton

RELEASE DATE:
November 25, 1998

RATED:
G
General Audiences

RUNTIME:
1 hour,
35 minutes

Saw it! ☐ Rating: ☆☆☆☆☆
Date: ___ / ___ / _____ With: _____
Notes: _____
_____

2 ACADEMY AWARDS

THE INCREDIBLES

DIRECTOR:
Brad Bird

RELEASE DATE:
November 5, 2004

RATED:
PG
for action violence

RUNTIME:
1 hour, 55 minutes

THE STORY

Posing as a regular family under the Superhero Relocation Program, the Incredibles are famous superheroes trying to fit in with normal folks. Bob (Craig T. Nelson) and Helen (Holly Hunter), formerly Mr. Incredible and Elastigirl, and their kids, Violet (Sarah Vowell), Dashiell (Spencer Fox), and Jack-Jack (Eli Fucile, Maeve Andrews) are now known as the Parr family. The government forced all supers into leading normal lives due to the collateral damage and lawsuits caused by their heroics. Helen becomes a mom raising her kids, Violet uses her force field bubbles to hide from bullying kids at school, and Dash has to slow down at school track meets so his break-neck speed won't raise suspicions. Bob has a desk job—and he hates it. His old pal, Frozone (Samuel L. Jackson) is also a relocated superhero. They secretly sneak out at night to fight crime, telling their wives they're just bowling. But evil is everywhere! A robot named Omnidroid 7, created by one of Mr. Incredible's former fans, Syndrome (Jason Lee), wants to kill all of the superheroes. Once again, it's up to the Incredibles to save the world!

DID YOU KNOW?
After a search for someone to voice Edna Mode failed, Brad Bird decided to voice her himself.

WATCH OUT FOR

The Incredibles is the first full-length CGI (computer-generated animation) movie to feature all human characters. Take special notice of Violet's long flowing hair. This was a huge technical achievement!

Saw it! ☐ Rating: ☆☆☆☆☆
Date: ___/___/_____ With: _____
Notes: _____
_____

UP

2 ACADEMY AWARDS

THE STORY

After Carl Fredricksen's wife dies, he becomes a recluse who doesn't want to leave his house. Now a retired balloon maker, Carl (Ed Asner) dreams of taking a trip to Paradise Falls in South America, a journey he and his wife had planned to take together. They wanted to visit the place where the famous explorer Charles F. Muntz (Christopher Plummer) claims he discovered a large, strange bird. When crabby old Mr. Fredricksen is about to be forced into a retirement home, he escapes using thousands of colorful balloons to lift his house into the sky! Young Wilderness Explorer Russell (Jordan Nagai) is standing on Carl's porch about to knock on the door when the entire house takes flight. A 78-year-old and an 8-year-old aren't the best traveling buddies, but they manage to survive a storm and make it to Paradise Falls. They meet a talking dog named Dug (Squirrel!), and a rare 13-foot-tall bird that Russell affectionately names Kevin. After an angry pack of dogs leads them to their master, they discover the mysterious owner is Muntz himself! But Muntz isn't who Carl thought he was, and when Muntz turns on the travelers, the only way to escape the villain is to get the house airborne again. Can they do this without balloons?

DID YOU KNOW?

Up was the first Disney movie (and the first 3-D animated film) to open the Cannes Film Festival in France.

DIRECTORS: Pete Docter and Bob Peterson

RELEASE DATE: May 29, 2009

RATED: **PG** for mild peril and action

RUNTIME: 1 hour, 36 minutes

Saw it! ☐ Rating: ☆☆☆☆☆

Date: ___ / ___ / _____ With: _____

Notes: _____

_____

24

A CHRISTMAS STORY

DIRECTOR:
Bob Clark

RELEASE DATE:
November 18, 1983

RATED:
PG
for strong language

RUNTIME:
1 hour, 34 minutes

THE STORY

A Christmas Story is a classic comedy about an all-American family living in the Midwest. Mrs. Parker (Melinda Dillon) is the pillar of the family in the face of calamity; the Old Man, whom they call Mr. Parker (Darren McGavin), is obsessed with the failing furnace; and 9-year-old Ralphie (Peter Billingsley) and his brother face bullies at school and deal with double- and triple-dog dares. The family's quirky nature brings the holiday season into perspective for Ralphie, as he pines for a Red Ryder Carbine Action 200-Shot Range Model Air Rifle for Christmas.

WHY IT'S FAMOUS

This seemingly typical family is affectionately known for its pretty unusual behavior. When all Ralphie wants for Christmas is a Red Ryder BB gun, the adults all tell him the same thing, "You'll shoot your eye out!" But he can't imagine anything better than that BB gun! Things take a bizarre turn when Mr. Parker wins a major prize—a lamp shaped like a woman's leg. Mrs. Parker doesn't like it one bit! She also doesn't like Ralphie to swear. *A Christmas Story* is a go-to family film for the season that brings some sense to the craziness of the holidays.

DID YOU KNOW?
Ralphie Parker repeats the name of his most-wanted Christmas present, a Red Ryder Carbine Action 200-Shot Range Model Air Rifle, 28 times during the movie. Count them yourself!

Saw it! ☐ Rating: ☆☆☆☆☆

Date: ___ / ___ / _____ With: _____

Notes: _____

_____

THE NIGHTMARE BEFORE CHRISTMAS

What do you get when you combine Halloween, Christmas, and Tim Burton? *The Nightmare Before Christmas!* Although Tim Burton did not direct this film, he wrote the story, produced the film, and created its unique-looking characters.

THE STORY

This stop motion animated musical is about a well-intentioned skeleton from Halloween Town who takes over Christmas and poses as Santa Claus, aka "Sandy Claws." He delivers gruesome toys on Christmas Eve, scaring the kids of Christmas Town in the process.

Jack Skellington is the Pumpkin King of Halloween Town. He's in charge of organizing the annual Halloween celebration for the citizens, a creepy collection of ghouls, goblins, vampires, and other monsters. Tired of doing the same thing year after year, Jack wants to do something more meaningful. Strolling through the forest one night, he enters Christmas Town through a portal. He sees how the people there are happily preparing for their annual holiday. Santa even has cheerful helpers—unlike the gloomy folks of Halloween Town! Jack wants to take part in the Christmas celebrations as well, so he decides to kidnap Santa and take his place! Although Jack's intentions are good, the Pumpkin King's experience lies more with spooky Halloween traditions than with the quaint, friendly customs of the winter holiday.

DID YOU KNOW?

The Nightmare Before Christmas took three years to complete. It took a week to shoot only one minute of the stop motion movie.

DIRECTOR:
Henry Selick

RELEASE DATE:
October 29, 1993

RATED:
PG
for some scary images

RUNTIME:
1 hour, 16 minutes

Saw it! ☐ Rating: ☆☆☆☆☆

Date: ___/___/_____ With: _____

Notes: _____

_____

26

THE GOONIES

DIRECTOR:
Richard
Donner

RELEASE DATE:
June 7, 1985

RATED:
PG
for adult situations
and language,
violence

RUNTIME:
1 hour,
54 minutes

THE STORY

A band of preteen boys call themselves "Goonies" because they live in an Oregon neighborhood called the Goon Docks. Their families are being forced to move out of their homes to make way for a country club to be built on the land, and they're desperate to save their homes. While

"Goonies never say die!" —Mikey Walsh

hanging out in their friend Mike Walsh's (Sean Astin) house one last time, the boys decide to snoop around the attic, where they discover an old treasure map belonging to a pirate named One-Eyed Willy. The nonstop adventure begins when they follow the clues, leading them to a secret cave and bringing them face-to-face with criminals!

   The map leads them to a cavern under a restaurant used by the delinquent Fratelli family to make counterfeit money. The Fratellis manage to capture Chunk (Jeff Cohen), the chubby clown of the gang, and squeeze him for information about the other kids' whereabouts. He spills the beans, telling the thieves about his pals' treasure hunt. After overcoming a series of traps left by pirates to protect the booty, the kids find One-Eyed Willy's long-lost pirate ship, but unknowingly lead the Fratelli family to the treasure too. Time is running out, and the country club builders are demanding to begin construction. Can this group of clever kids escape the clutches of the wicked Fratelli family and find the treasure while saving their homes?

STARRING:
Sean Astin,
Josh Brolin,
Jeff Cohen,
and Corey
Feldman

**SCREEN-
PLAY
WRITTEN
BY:**
Chris
Columbus

**FILM
LOCATION:**
Astoria,
Oregon

DID YOU KNOW?
Chris Columbus, the writer of *The Goonies* screenplay, later directed three of the *Harry Potter* movies: *Sorcerer's Stone*, *Chamber of Secrets*, and *Prisoner of Azkaban*.

Saw it! ☐ Rating: ☆☆☆☆☆
Date: ___/___/_____ With: _____
Notes: _____
_____

27

HOW THE GRINCH STOLE CHRISTMAS

DIRECTOR:
Ron Howard

RELEASE DATE:
November 17, 2000

RATED:
PG
for some crude humor

RUNTIME:
1 hour,
44 minutes

Theodor Geisel, also known as Dr. Seuss, is the author and illustrator of the book *How the Grinch Stole Christmas* (1957). His unique characters from the book are recreated in human form in the movie of the same title, *How the Grinch Stole Christmas*, which was released in 2000. The original animated short film was made for television in 1966.

THE STORY

The Grinch (Jim Carrey) and his faithful dog Max live in a dark cave on a snow-covered mountaintop high above Whoville. The cheerful town below is preparing for Christmas, and the Whos laugh and sing as they put up

elaborate decorations and gather food for the huge celebration. The Grinch, who has a heart "two sizes too small," doesn't like all the hustle and bustle of the season. The racket and over-the-top decorations are too much for him, and he decides this year to stop Christmas from coming.

Speeding down the steep mountain on a sleigh with Max dressed as a reindeer, the Grinch hatches the perfect plan to disguise himself as Santa Claus—but instead of delivering presents, the green Santa will take everything away, including their favorite dinner, the great roast beast! On Christmas Eve, the Grinch slides down each chimney stealing everything, but one tiny Who, Cindy Lou Who (Taylor Momsen), catches him in the evil act. After fooling Cindy Lou, he escapes with all the trimmings of Whoville's Christmas piled on his sleigh and rides back to his cave. Convinced he'll hear the sound of disappointment coming from Whoville on Christmas morning, the Grinch is shocked to hear just the opposite.

WHY IT'S FAMOUS

How The Grinch Stole Christmas continues to teach a universal message: the true meaning of the season lives in our hearts.

STARRING:
Jim Carey,
Jeffrey Tambor,
and
Christine
Baranski

**BOX
OFFICE:**
$345.1
million

MUSIC:
James Horner

DID YOU KNOW?
How the Grinch Stole Christmas was the first
Dr. Seuss book to be made into a full-length motion picture.

Saw it! ☐ Rating: ☆☆☆☆☆
Date: ___ / ___ / _____ With: _____
Notes: _____
_____

28

EDWARD SCISSORHANDS

DIRECTOR:
Tim Burton

RELEASE DATE:
December 14, 1990

RATED:
PG-13
for suggestive humor, some teen drinking, and language

RUNTIME:
1 hour,
45 minutes

THE STORY

This film begins with a grandmother telling her granddaughter a story about where snow comes from. She tells her about a young man named Edward (Johnny Depp). As a result of his inventor's (Vincent Price) sudden death, Edward, a gothic Frankenstein-like human, is left with large scissors for hands. He grows up isolated, hiding in a dark castle perched on a hill overlooking a cheerful suburban residential area. One day, the local Avon Lady, Peg Boggs, comes calling at the castle. She sees that the speechless young man dressed all in black is alone and decides he's harmless. She takes Edward into her home where her daughter Kim (Winona Ryder), eventually falls in love with him. He becomes popular with some people because he trims hedges and hair with flair! To show his love, Edward uses his hands to create an ice sculpture of Kim. As he's working, the shaved ice flies into the sky and falls like snow. But this love story is not meant to be. Edward's hands cause havoc with the neighbors and the town wants him gone. Edward retreats to his dark castle and is never seen again. Kim, now an old woman, tells her granddaughter that the only sign he's still alive is the yearly snow that still falls over the town.

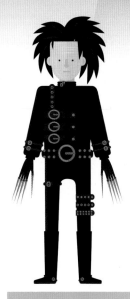

DID YOU KNOW?
This film was the first-ever collaboration between Johnny Depp and Tim Burton. They have since made 8 films together over a span of 25 years.

Saw it! ☐ Rating: ☆☆☆☆☆
Date: ___/___/_____ With: _____
Notes: _____
_____

FLY AWAY HOME

THE STORY

Amy Alden (Anna Paquin) and her mother are in a car accident in New Zealand. Amy survives, but her mother doesn't. Her parents are divorced. Her father, Thomas Alden (Jeff Daniels), is a sculptor and inventor who lives in Ontario, Canada. After the accident, Amy leaves New Zealand to live with her dad. Things are awkward at first, especially when her dad's girlfriend, Susan (Dana Delany), is around. One day, Amy finds some goose eggs and takes them home. She hides them in a drawer in the barn. When the eggs hatch, the first thing the chicks see is Amy, and now they think she's their mother! Amy's dad lets her keep the chicks as pets; however, the birds need to migrate for the winter. Without a mother to teach them how to fly, they may not survive. The game warden tells the Aldens they can't keep the geese unless their wings are clipped so they can't fly. Thomas figures out that the birds can be taught to fly, and since the chicks already follow Amy around everywhere, they'll likely follow her up into the sky too. He makes a special homemade light aircraft and teaches Amy how to fly the machine, turning Amy into a human Mother Goose!

WHY IT'S FAMOUS

Fly Away Home is loosely based on the real-life events of William Lishman and his daughter Carmen. In 1993, Lishman led 16 birds from Ontario to Virginia. The following year, 13 geese returned.

DIRECTOR:
Carroll Ballard

RELEASE DATE:
September 13, 1996

RATED:
PG
for an opening accident scene and some mild language

RUNTIME:
1 hour, 47 minutes

Saw it! ☐ Rating: ☆☆☆☆☆
Date: ___ / ___ / _____ With: _____
Notes: _____
_____

30

THE PRINCESS BRIDE

DIRECTOR:
Rob Reiner

RELEASE DATE:
October 9, 1987

RATED:
PG
for adult situations/ language

RUNTIME:
1 hour, 38 minutes

THE STORY

An old man reads a story to his grandson, who is home sick from school. Buttercup (Robin Wright) lives on a farm in the fictional country of Florin. Her loyal farm boy, Westley (Cary Elwes), loves her and always answers her commands with, "As you wish." Buttercup realizes that she also loves Westley, but before they can get married, Westley sails away to seek his fortune. His ship is attacked by the Dread Pirate Roberts, and no one survives. Five years later, Buttercup is engaged to marry Prince Humperdinck (Chris Sarandon). Before the wedding, Buttercup is kidnapped by an odd trio: Vizzini (Wallace Shawn), Fezzik (André the Giant), and a Spanish fencer Inigo Montoya (Mandy Patinkin) who wants to avenge his father, who was killed by a six-fingered man. Montoya practices for revenge by repeating, "Hello, my name is Inigo Montoya. You killed my father. Prepare to die."

DID YOU KNOW?
This film made the American Film Institute's 100 Greatest Love Stories.

Meanwhile, along with a mysterious masked man, the prince goes after the outlaws who took Buttercup. Atop the Cliffs of Insanity, the masked man defeats Montoya in a swordfight and crushes the band of outlaws. He grabs Buttercup and tells her that he is the Dread Pirate Roberts. Thinking he killed her beloved Westley, Buttercup pushes him down a hill. As he falls he yells, "As you wish!" The grandson asks his grandfather to read the story again. The ending will answer all your questions too!

Saw it! ☐ Rating: ☆☆☆☆☆
Date: ___/____/_____ With: _____
Notes: _____
_____

THE SECRET GARDEN

THE STORY

Mary Lennox (Kate Maberly) lives in India with her parents, where she is cared for by a nanny and servants. One day, tragedy strikes and her parents are killed in an earthquake. Now an orphan, Mary is shipped off to England to live with her uncle, Lord Archibald (John Lynch), at Misselthwaite Manor in Yorkshire. Lord Archibald's wife died many years before, and heartbroken, he has since spent his days traveling, away from the manor. Mrs. Medlock (Maggie Smith) manages the estate and looks after Lord Archibald's son and Mary's cousin, Colin, a 9-year-old sickly, bedridden boy. A boy named Dickon Sowerby, a relative of one of the manor servants, befriends Mary. With Dickon's help, Mary discovers a hidden garden on the castle grounds and the key that unlocks the garden's door. Mary and Dickon inspire Colin to walk and show him that happiness can be found.

WHY IT'S FAMOUS

This British film is based on the 1911 book by Frances Hodgson Burnett, which was inspired by her own life experiences.

DID YOU KNOW?

A fountain dedicated to Burnett at the Conservatory Garden in New York City's Central Park is said to be of the two main characters in *The Secret Garden*, Mary and Dickon.

DIRECTOR:
Agnieszka Holland

RELEASE DATE:
August 13, 1993

RATED:

G

General Audiences

RUNTIME:
1 hour, 41 minutes

Saw it! ☐ Rating: ☆☆☆☆☆
Date: ___/___/_____ With: _____
Notes: _____
_____

32

PRIDE & PREJUDICE

DIRECTOR:
Joe Wright

**RELEASE
DATE:**
November 23,
2005

RATED:
PG
for some mild
thematic elements

RUNTIME:
2 hours,
9 minutes

THE STORY

Five sisters live in the British countryside with their parents, Mr. Bennet (Donald Sutherland) and Mrs. Bennet (Brenda Blethyn): Jane (Rosamund Pike), Elizabeth (Keira Knightley), Mary (Talula Riley), Kitty (Carey Mulligan), and Lydia (Jena Malone). It's their mother's business to marry off her daughters, and she must find a suitable suitor for each one, starting with the oldest. Back then, marriage was only a matter of money—love was expected to gradually form over time. Mr. Bingley (Simon Woods), an eligible bachelor with a substantial income, moves near the Bennet's country home, and Mrs. Bennet begins to scheme about how to introduce him to her daughters. Mr. Bingley brings his friend Mr. Darcy (Matthew Macfadyen) to a local dance, and the two meet Jane and her sister Elizabeth. Jane and Mr. Bingley like each other right away, but Mr. Darcy does not like Lizzy because she is from a lower class. He carelessly voices his opinion of Elizabeth within earshot and tells Mr. Bingley that she is "tolerable, but not handsome enough to tempt me." Lizzy, a stubborn woman who knows what she wants, swears she will hate Mr. Darcy forever. This film marvelously wraps you up in the complicated courtships indicative of this time. Will Mr. Darcy and Elizabeth learn to let go of their pride and the inherent prejudices of their society?

STARRING:
Keira Knightley, Matthew Macfadyen, Brenda Blethyn, and Donald Sutherland

ORIGINAL STORY BY:
Jane Austen

FILM LOCATION:
England

DID YOU KNOW?

Pride & Prejudice is based on a Jane Austen novel published in 1813. Although Austen wrote about love and marriage, she never married herself.

Saw it! ☐ Rating: ☆☆☆☆☆
Date: ___/___/_____ With: _____
Notes: _____
_____

33

DESPICABLE ME

DIRECTORS:
Pierre Coffin
and
Chris Renaud

RELEASE DATE:
July 9, 2010

RATED:
PG
for rude humor
and mild action

RUNTIME:
1 hour,
35 minutes

THE STORY

Gru (Steve Carell) is a grumpy supervillain anxious to recapture his glory as the world's best villain. His fellow villain, Vector (Jason Segel), has stolen the Great Pyramid of Giza and become top dog in the world of evil. Gru cooks up a plan to steal the moon, but he first needs an influx of cash to invent a powerful shrink ray. Gru borrows money from the Bank of Evil, and together with his army of irresistibly cute minions, they create the shrink ray—only to have Vector take it from them. Enraged, Gru adopts three orphan girls, Margo (Miranda Cosgrove), Edith (Dana Gaier), and Agnes (Elsie Fisher) to use them for a wicked plan. Posing as Girl Scouts selling cookies, Gru plans to use the girls to fool Vector into letting them into his house to steal back the shrink ray—and it works! Gru successfully shrinks and steals the moon. While in his care, the adorable girls run amuck at Gru's house, and amid the chaos,

Gru and the girls start to feel like a family. However, Vector kidnaps the girls and offers to trade them for the moon. Will Gru save the girls from Vector's diabolical hands?

This 3-D film also includes the comedy voice talents of Will Arnett, Ken Jeong, Kristin Wiig, Russell Brand, and Danny McBride.

UP NEXT

The success of this film led to the sequel *Despicable Me 2* (2013), as well as the spin-off movie *Minions* (2015). *Despicable Me 3* is set to hit theaters in 2017.

STARRING:
Steve Carell, Jason Segel, Miranda Cosgrove, and Russell Brand

BOX OFFICE:
$543.1 million

DID YOU KNOW?

Pharrell Williams produced *Despicable Me*'s soundtrack. Williams also wrote, produced, and performed "Happy" for the *Despicable Me 2* film soundtrack.

MUSIC:
Songs by Hans Zimmer and Pharrell Williams

Saw it! ☐ Rating: ☆☆☆☆☆

Date: ___/___/_____ With: _____

Notes: _____

_____

34

ICE AGE

DIRECTORS:
Chris Wedge
and Carlos
Saldanha

**RELEASE
DATE**:
March 15, 2002

RATED:
PG
for mild peril

RUNTIME:
1 hour,
21 minutes

THE STORY

This digitally animated movie follows three prehistoric animals that find a human baby and make a pact to return him to his family. Manny (Ray Romano), a warm hearted woolly mammoth; Sid (John Leguizamo), a fast-talking sloth; and Diego (Denis Leary), a menacing saber-toothed tiger, bond as they cross the frozen tundra, going in the opposite direction of the seasonal animal migration. Along their cold and comedic journey, you'll see amazing scenes of snow-covered mountains, glistening glaciers, and expansive land during the Ice Age. The movie also follows an out-of-control, long-toothed squirrel named Scrat. Scrat is desperately trying to gather food for the winter, but faces many hilarious, terrifying obstacles in an effort to save his prized acorn—which is about as big as he is!

UP NEXT

Get ready for an *Ice Age* marathon, because this film became a franchise with three more films: *Ice Age: The Meltdown* (2006), *Ice Age: Dawn of the Dinosaurs* (2009), and *Ice Age: Continental Drift* (2012). *Ice Age 5* is set to hit theaters in 2016.

DID YOU KNOW?

After 40 different attempts, John Leguizamo came up with Sid's voice watching documentaries about sloths. He learned that these slow animals store food in their cheek pouches. To mimic the sound, the actor put a sandwich in his mouth and tried to talk!

Saw it! ☐ Rating: ☆☆☆☆☆

Date: ___ / ___ / _____ With: _____

Notes: _____

_____

SHREK

THE STORY

Shrek (Mike Myers) is an ogre living alone in his swamp, and he likes it that way. But one day, his peace and quiet is interrupted by a group of fairy tale characters—the Three Little Pigs, the Three Blind Mice, the Gingerbread Man, and Pinocchio, among others—who show up and ask Shrek for help. The mean, power-hungry Lord Farquaad (John Lithgow) kicked them out of the kingdom, and they don't have anywhere to live. Farquaad asks the Magic Mirror for a bride to choose from: Cinderella, Snow White, or Princess Fiona (Cameron Diaz)—who's cursed, lives in a tower, and turns into an ogre at night. The Magic Mirror tries to tell Farquaad this small detail, but he doesn't listen! The fast-talking Donkey (Eddie Murphy) joins Shrek on the way to Duloc to talk to Farquaad. When they arrive, Shrek and Farquaad make a deal: The ogre slays the dragon, rescues Fiona from the tower, and brings her to him. In exchange, Farquaad will ban the fairy tale creatures from Shrek's swamp.

WATCH OUT FOR

Two sequels followed, *Shrek 2* (2004) and *Shrek the Third* (2007).

DID YOU KNOW?

Mike Myers asked to re-record all of his lines in the Scottish accent he learned from his mom when she read him bedtime stories when he was young!

DIRECTORS:
Andrew Adamson and Vicky Jenson

RELEASE DATE:
May 18, 2001

RATED:
PG
mild language and some crude humor

RUNTIME:
1 hour, 30 minutes

Saw it! ☐ Rating: ☆☆☆☆☆

Date: ___/___/_____ With: _____

Notes: _____

_____

36

DRUMLINE

DIRECTOR:
Charles Stone III

RELEASE DATE:
December 13, 2002

RATED:
PG-13
for innuendo and language

RUNTIME:
1 hour, 58 minutes

THE STORY

Devon (Nick Cannon) is an African-American teenager from Harlem with a big attitude and an even bigger desire for success. He scores a full scholarship to the fictitious A&T University in Atlanta, Georgia, to play drums in the marching band. Devon likes to show off, but band director Dr. Lee Jones (Orlando Jones) is more traditional; his players need to know how to read music, play a variety of classics, and work as a team: "One band, one sound." Devon is more interested in Laila (Zoe Saldana), the dance team captain, than in teamwork. Problems begin when he antagonizes the section leader and news gets out that he can't read music. Devon gets demoted within the drumline and is eventually kicked out of the band. However, the school's president tells Dr. Lee that they need to win the BET television-sponsored Big Southern Classic competition. He needs to modernize the band's sound or he's out! Devon's slick drum moves earn him a spot back in the band to help beat their rivals (and real band champions) Morris Brown College.

DID YOU KNOW?

The Georgia Superdome was filled with 50,000 extras to film the final drumoff. The marching bands from Morris Brown College, Clark Atlanta University, Bethune-Cookman University, and Grambling State University are featured in the scene.

Saw it! ☐ Rating: ☆☆☆☆☆
Date: ___/___/_____ With: _____
Notes: _____
_____

WHALE RIDER

THE STORY

A 12-year-old Maori girl named Pai (Keisha Castle-Hughes) lives in present-day New Zealand and wants to become the leader of her people, which is traditionally a man's role. After her twin brother and mother die during childbirth, the little girl is named Paikea, after a mythic ancestor of the Maoris. According to legend, Paikea led the tribe to settle in Whangara by riding a whale. Since then, descendants of the great leader have become tribe chiefs, and the name Paikea is reserved for the first-born male of a family. Pai's dad, Porourangi (Cliff Curtis), is an artist and leaves New Zealand, leaving Pai to be raised by her grandparents: Koro (Rawiri Paratene), the leader of the tribe, and Nanny Flowers (Vicky Haughton). One day, Koro gathers all of the teenage boys to teach them how to be a Maori. Pai is not invited. As you can imagine, she is disappointed. However, this movie is anything but disappointing—the ending is so surprising that whatever you might guess, you'll likely be surprised.

Whale Rider shows us the struggle native cultures face to maintain traditions, and that girls have the ability to be strong leaders!

DID YOU KNOW?

Keisha Castle-Hughes had never acted before *Whale Rider*. She was 13 years old when she was nominated for the Academy Award for Best Actress in a Leading Role, the youngest actress ever nominated for an Oscar in this category.

DIRECTOR:
Niki Caro

RELEASE DATE:
August 29, 2003 (USA)

RATED:

PG-13

for brief language and a momentary drug reference

RUNTIME:
1 hour, 41 minutes

Saw it! ☐ Rating: ☆☆☆☆☆

Date: ___/___/_____ With: _____

Notes: _____

_____

38

THE CHRONICLES OF NARNIA: THE LION, THE WITCH AND THE WARDROBE

DIRECTOR:
Andrew Adamson

RELEASE DATE:
December 9, 2005

RATED:
PG
for battle sequences and frightening moments

RUNTIME:
2 hours,
23 minutes

THE STORY

In this first film, Peter (William Moseley), Susan (Anna Popplewell), Edmund (Skandar Keynes), and Lucy Pevensie (Georgie Henley) are evacuated from London to save them from Nazi raids during World War II. They move in with Professor Kirke (Jim Broadbent) at his vast home in the English countryside. Playing hide-and-seek, Lucy stumbles upon a wardrobe that leads to the magical land of Narnia, a parallel fantasy world. She shows her siblings the portal, and they all travel through the closet into a snow-covered land inhabited by strange creatures. Narnia has been cast in a perpetual winter for a century by a spell from the evil White Witch (Tilda Swinton). The children meet Aslan (Liam Neeson), a talking lion, and together they set out to hunt down the White Witch. Can the Pevensies defeat the White Witch and return to reality?

UP NEXT

Two more books in the series were turned into movies, *Prince Caspian* (2008) and *The Voyage of the Dawn Treader* (2010).

DID YOU KNOW?

Clive Staples Lewis, better known as C.S. Lewis, wrote the seven-book series *The Chronicles of Narnia*. He taught at Oxford University in England along with his colleague and good friend, J.R.R. Tolkien, who wrote *The Lord of the Rings* trilogy.

Saw it! ☐ Rating: ☆☆☆☆☆

Date: ___/___/_____ With: _____

Notes: _____

_____

WHERE THE WILD THINGS ARE

This movie is adapted from Maurice Sendak's beloved 1963 children's tale *Where the Wild Things Are*. The entire book consists of 10 sentences — that's 37 pages or 388 words. The reader's imagination is left to interpret the author's muted drawings to get the whole story. Now this abbreviated classic is a feature-length motion picture.

DIRECTOR:
Spike Jonze

THE STORY

Max (Max Records) is a mischievous 9-year-old boy who escapes his complicated home life by hiding in his imagination. After an argument with his sister and throwing a tantrum in front of his mom, Max goes to his room, throws on a wolf costume, and travels on a boat to an island inhabited by The Wild Things: Carol (James Gandolfini), Ira (Forest Whitaker), Judith (Catherine O'Hara), Alexander (Paul Dano), Douglas (Chris Cooper), and K.W (Lauren Ambrose). The horned, 10-foot-tall monster-like creatures accept Max as their king because he promises to use his magic to help them solve their problems—something Max wishes he were able to do in his real life.

DID YOU KNOW?
Max Records was 8 years old when he was chosen for the role of Max.

RELEASE DATE:
October 16, 2009

RATED:
PG
for mild thematic elements, some adventure action, and brief language

WATCH OUT FOR

To convincingly re-create the story's furry creatures for the film, the director used a combination of live people inside costumes and computer animation.

RUNTIME:
1 hour, 41 minutes

Saw it! ☐ Rating: ☆☆☆☆☆
Date: ___/___/_____ With: _____
Notes: _____
_____

40

HAPPY FEET

DIRECTOR:
George Miller,
Warren Coleman,
and Judy Morris

RELEASE DATE:
November 17, 2006

RATED:
PG
for some mild peril
and rude humor

RUNTIME:
1 hour,
48 minutes

THE STORY

Mumble (Elijah Wood) is born without a proper "heartsong," the sounds penguins make to attract a mate. Mumble's parents, Norma Jean (Nicole Kidman) and Memphis (Hugh Jackman) worry that without it he may never find true love. However, Mumble has a special talent: He can tap dance like no other Emperor Penguin in the colony! But since Mumble is simply too strange to be part of Emperor Land, Noah the elder penguin banishes him and his "hippity-hoppity" feet. Drifting alone across the white landscape, Mumble meets the Adelies, a joyful trio of penguins. They're impressed with his moves and Ramon (Robin Williams), leader of these misfit penguins, invites Mumble to party with them. However, when Mumble ends up confined at Marine World in Australia, all hope for his return home seems lost. Can Mumble go back to his arctic habitat and find a mate in spite of the odds set against him?

Happy Feet sends a valuable message. One penguin shows up with a set of plastic six-pack rings around his neck and a seagull wearing a yellow band on his leg claims he was "tagged by aliens." These references to humans' intrusion on the environment are wrapped up in this movie's broader message about acceptance and being unique.

DID YOU KNOW?
Tony Award-winning dancer Savion Glover, was responsible for the dance sequences in *Happy Feet*.

UP NEXT
Happy Feet 2 followed in 2011.

Saw it! ☐ Rating: ☆☆☆☆☆
Date: ___/ ___/ _____ With: _____
Notes: _____
_____

THE LEGO® MOVIE

THE STORY

In this original computer-animated movie, construction worker Legos band together to battle against the evil Lord Business (Will Ferrell). Vitruvius (Morgan Freeman), a wise Lego wizard, prophesies that whoever finds the Piece of Resistance is "The Special"—the chosen one destined to save the Lego universe from a superweapon called the Kragle. Emmet (Chris Pratt) is a construction worker who encounters Wyldstyle (Elizabeth Banks) scavenging on the construction site. He tries to help her and falls into a hole where the Piece of Resistance attaches to his back. Wyldstyle takes Emmet to Vitruvius, where he learns they are both Master Builders, meaning they don't need instructions to build. They must battle Lord Business because he wants to destroy their creativity. Emmet recalls a vision he had of "The Man Upstairs," a human who glues his Lego creations after building them by following the instructions. Emmet encourages the Legos to work as a team to defeat him. Can the Lego people use their creativity to defeat Lord Business? Will Emmet reach the real world in time?

DID YOU KNOW?

Inspired by these classic building blocks, Legoland® operates seven theme parks around the world. Two are located in the United States, in California and Florida.

DIRECTORS:
Phil Lord and Christopher Miller

RELEASE DATE:
February 7, 2014

RATED:
PG
for mild action and rude humor

RUNTIME:
1 hour, 40 minutes

Saw it! ☐ Rating: ☆☆☆☆☆
Date: ___/___/_____ With: _____
Notes: _____
_____

42 WRECK-IT RALPH

DIRECTOR:
Rich Moore

RELEASE DATE:
November 2, 2012

RATED:
PG
for some rude humor and mild action/violence

RUNTIME:
1 hour, 41 minutes

THE STORY

Nicelanders don't like Wreck-It Ralph (John C. Reilly). He destroys everything in the Fix-It Felix Jr. game because that's what he's coded to do! Felix (Jack McBrayer) fixes what Ralph destroys. After being the bad guy for 30 years, Ralph decides to get advice from a video game villains' support group. They tell him he can't change the game's program. Disappointed, he leaves the game world of Niceland through the electric cables in search of a medal from the new Hero's Duty video game—everyone loves heroes! Sgt. Calhoun (Jane Lynch) is getting ready to attack a player when Ralph arrives, accidentally shoots the player, and ends the game. He sees a medal hanging in midair and grabs it, but then accidentally steps on a Cy-Bug egg that tries to attack him. He escapes to the Sugar Rush game next and then jumps from game to game trying to escape attacks and gain a medal. In the meantime, a girl tries to play Fix-It Felix Jr., but the game doesn't work because Ralph is missing. She reports the game is out of order, and the arcade owner plans to pull the plug on it the next day. Fearing this, Felix leaves his game to find Ralph. Can Felix find Ralph in time, and will Ralph finally earn the respect he desires?

DID YOU KNOW?
The British Royal Wedding influenced the Nicelanders' outfits since it was big news in 2011 when the characters were being designed.

Saw it! ☐ Rating: ☆☆☆☆☆
Date: ___/___/_____ With: _____
Notes: _____
_____

1 ACADEMY AWARD

MRS. DOUBTFIRE

THE STORY

Mrs. Doubtfire is secretly a mister! Daniel Hillard (Robin Williams) is a divorced father of three. He's an unemployed voice actor who loves his children very much. However, he's also a rather irresponsible adult. He prefers to play with his kids rather than discipline them. Miranda Hillard (Sally Field), the children's mother, needs a nanny to care for the kids while she's at work. Daniel can't stand the thought of seeing his kids only one day a week, so without telling his ex-wife, he comes up with the perfect solution—he decides to become their nanny. With help from his brother, a professional makeup artist, Daniel transforms himself from a fun-loving dad into a stern British nanny—and the whole family adores him…umm, her! Mrs. Doubtfire cooks, cleans, and helps with homework. Only Miranda's boyfriend Stu (Pierce Brosnan) thinks the nanny is a bit strange, but otherwise no one has a clue about the disguise. However, after several close calls, Mrs. Doubtfire forgets to shut the door to the bathroom and one of the kids sees "her" do something weird—and Daniel's cover is blown! What happens next? You'll have to watch *Mrs. Doubtfire* to find out.

DID YOU KNOW?

It took four hours to put the heavy makeup on Robin Williams that transformed him into Mrs. Doubtfire.

DIRECTOR:
Chris Columbus

RELEASE DATE:
November 24, 1993

RATED:
PG-13
for some sexual references

RUNTIME:
2 hours, 5 minutes

Saw it! ☐   Rating: ☆☆☆☆☆

Date: ___ / ___ / _____   With: _____

Notes: _____

_____

44

FORREST GUMP

DIRECTOR:
Robert Zemeckis

RELEASE DATE:
July 6, 1994

RATED:
PG-13
for drug content,
some sensuality,
and war violence

RUNTIME:
2 hours,
22 minutes

"Momma always said life was like a box of chocolates. You never know what you're gonna get." —Forrest Gump

THE STORY

Forrest Gump (Tom Hanks) is a slow, naïve but honest man who lives in Alabama. While waiting at the bus stop, Forrest starts telling his life story to the riders waiting next to him. His mother (Sally Field) told him simple truths as a child, such as "Stupid is as stupid does," and encouraged him to be proud of himself no matter how the world treated him. He recounts how he wore leg braces as a kid and was bullied for being a cripple. One day, bullies surrounded and threatened him. His best friend Jenny (Robin Wright) screamed, "Run, Forrest! Run!" He ran so fast that his leg braces flew right off his legs.

This is how Forrest ends up with a college football scholarship. From this point on, specifically between 1950 and 1980, Forrest is somehow involved in every major American historical event. He's awarded the Medal of Honor for his service in Vietnam, becomes a ping-pong champion, and later a millionaire after he and his friend, Lieutenant Dan (Gary Sinise), invest in "some kind of fruit company" called Apple. But does he find true love?

WHY IT'S FAMOUS

This charming film takes a look at our own culture and history. While Forrest's life takes him to key moments in American history as a war veteran, we also glimpse what prominent 1960s subcultures were like through the eyes of Jenny, Forrest's love interest. She becomes a hippie and an anti-Vietnam war protester. We find ourselves desperately wanting Forrest to find love and happiness, and the bittersweet conclusion to this movie is very satisfying.

STARRING:
Tom Hanks,
Robin Wright,
Gary Sinise,
and Sally Field

BOX OFFICE:
$677.9 million

DID YOU KNOW?

Robert Zemeckis used real TV footage and inserted Forrest into the clips: Lyndon B. Johnson awarding Forrest the Medal of Honor; Forrest at college during George Wallace's Stand in the Schoolhouse Door; Forrest visiting Nixon at the White House; and Forrest at the Watergate Hotel. An interview with Dick Cavett even results in Forrest inspiring John Lennon to write the song "Imagine."

MUSIC:
Alan Silvestri

Saw it! ☐ Rating: ☆☆☆☆☆
Date: ___/___/_____ With: _____
Notes: _____
_____

45

THE RED BALLOON

DIRECTOR:
Albert Lamorisse

RELEASE DATE:
1956 (France);
March 11, 1957
(USA)

RATED:
G
General
Audiences

RUNTIME:
34 minutes

This short film has resonated with children for over half a century. *The Red Balloon*'s heartwarming, almost-silent script won the Oscar for Best Original Screenplay in 1957, making it the only short film to win an Academy Award outside of the short film categories.

THE STORY

A simple story about a boy who encounters a red balloon that starts following him around his Parisian neighborhood seems like a child's dream come true. A balloon that thinks and moves on its own? It's pure childhood imagination at its best! The fun soon turns

"LE BALLON ROUGE" (ORIGINAL TITLE) FRANCE

into a nuisance for Pascal, the young boy, when the red balloon starts causing commotion. In one instance, the pesky balloon even sneaks into his school and disrupts class! Pascal then meets a little girl with the same problem, except her balloon is blue. Pascal, Sabine, and their colorful balloons manage to have fun adventures in the dull and neglected streets of Paris. However, reality sets in for Pascal and his helium-filled friend when a bunch of bullies pop the red balloon, destroying Pascal's seemingly perfect dream. But don't worry, the young hero's sadness is lifted by a surprising twist, and his heart takes flight!

WHY IT'S FAMOUS

The Red Balloon is full of life lessons and visual splendor. Having a friend to count on and share what can sometimes be an overwhelming world with is special, like the friendship between Pascal and his balloon. This movie also serves as a reminder that some moments in life can seem magical! Taking place on the streets in Paris, the City of Lights, only adds to the visual experience of this enchanting movie.

DID YOU KNOW?

The two children featured in this movie are film director Albert Lamorisse's own son and daughter, Pascal and Sabine Lamorisse.

STARRING:
Pascal Lamorisse, Sabine Lamorisse, and Georges Sellier

SCORE BY:
Maurice Leroux

SCREEN-PLAY WRITTEN BY:
Albert Lamorisse

Saw it! ☐ Rating: ☆☆☆☆☆
Date: ___ / ___ / _____ With: _____
Notes: _____
_____

46

MY NEIGHBOR TOTORO "TONARI NO TOTORO" (ORIGINAL TITLE) JAPAN

DIRECTOR:
Hayao Miyazaki

RELEASE DATE:
April 16, 1988 (Japan);
May 7, 1993 (USA)

RATED:
G
General Audiences

RUNTIME:
1 hour,
26 minutes

THE STORY

Totoro is a friendly spirit that lives in an old camphor tree in the forest and can only be seen by children. Although Totoro is huge compared to the children that he encounters, this cute character is gentle and playful. When sisters Mei (Chika Sakamoto) and Satsuki (Noriko Hidaka) move to the Japanese countryside, they do what any curious child would do in a new neighborhood; they set out to explore their new surroundings. They discover magical creatures that take them on wild adventures.

WATCH OUT FOR

The animated characters in this beloved tale are a concept of the imaginative Japanese storyteller, Hayao Miyazaki. This film will introduce you to the world of Japanese animation, which is noticeably different from the American cartoon style. Though this movie does not rely on common American themes, it does have a little bit of everything: sadness, surprise, joy, and a lesson.

UP NEXT

Also from Miyazaki: *Kiki's Delivery Service* (1989), *Princes Mononoke* (1997), *Spirited Away* (2001), and *Ponyo* (2008). Disney's English-language adaptation of *My Neighbor Totoro* (2005) includes the voices of sisters Dakota and Elle Fanning as Satsuki and Mei. The Disney adaptation of *Ponyo* (2009) features the voices of Tina Fey, Cate Blanchett, Liam Neeson, Betty White, Lily Tomlin, Noah Cyrus (Miley Cyrus's brother), and Frankie Jonas (the youngest of the Jonas Brothers).

Saw it! ☐ Rating: ☆☆☆☆☆
Date: ___/ ___/ _____ With: _____
Notes: _____
_____

CHILDREN OF HEAVEN

"BACHEHA-YE ASEMAN" (ORIGINAL TITLE) IRAN

47

THE STORY

In a very poor area in the south of Tehran, Iran, 9-year-old Ali (Amir Farrokh Hashemian) picks up his sister's only pair of shoes from the cobbler and stops at the market on his way home. He puts the bag down to buy potatoes, but when he looks back down it's gone! A blind garbage collector mistook the bag for trash. In a panic, Ali goes home and tells 7-year-old Zahra (Bahare Seddiqi), what happened and begs her not to tell their parents. He's afraid to make their father angry. They agree to find a solution on their own and spare their parents more grief. However, the problem is a big one: Zahra doesn't have another pair of shoes to wear to school. Ali and Zahra agree to share Ali's sneakers; Zahra wears them to school in the morning, and at midday they switch, so Ali can wear them in the afternoon. A few days later, a solution materializes. There's a running competition with other schools coming up, and the third place prize is a new pair of sneakers. Ali just has to place third, and the problem will be solved!

Ali runs in the race, and the outcome surprises everyone!

DID YOU KNOW?

The director chose Amir Farrokh, who had never acted before, after seeing him crying in his classroom because he forgot his notebook. Majidi asked the boy why he was crying, and Amir lied and said he had amnesia, making him the perfect Ali!

DIRECTOR:
Majid Majidi

RELEASE DATE:
February 1997 (Iran);
January 22, 1999 (USA)

RATED:
PG
for some mild language

RUNTIME:
1 hour, 29 minutes

Saw it! ☐ Rating: ☆☆☆☆☆

Date: ___/___/_____ With: _____

Notes: _____

_____

48

CROUCHING TIGER, HIDDEN DRAGON

DIRECTOR:
Ang Lee

RELEASE DATE:
July 8, 2000
(China);
January 12, 2001
(USA)

RATED:

PG-13

for martial arts
violence and
some sexuality

RUNTIME:
2 hours

 4 ACADEMY AWARDS

"WO HU CANG LONG" (ORIGINAL TITLE)
AMERICAN-CHINESE CO-PRODUCTION

THE STORY

Emotions run very high in this powerful martial arts action drama about love, loyalty, and the conflicts that arise when these two feelings collide. *Crouching Tiger, Hidden Dragon* follows the pursuit of Green Destiny, a legendary holy sword stolen by an unlikely thief. This event unleashes a series of ambitious martial arts battles to recover the sword. Both male and female warriors engage in fights that look more like aerial acrobatics; the characters gracefully float high above bamboo trees and perform spectacular gravity-defying stunts.

WHY IT'S FAMOUS

Much of the captivating beauty of this motion picture is due to the breathtaking locations. From the remote corners of the Gobi Desert to the Anji bamboo forest in Jiangsu, China, the cinematography alone is worth watching. Most of the fight scenes were filmed with the actors, not stunt artists. Taiwanese director Ang Lee (*Life of Pi*, 2012) was proud of this accomplishment, since it's very uncommon to have actors suspended across 60-foot-high bamboo branches!

This film features daring stunts and fight sequences by the famous Chinese martial arts choreographer Youen Woo-ping. He is also responsible for the extraordinary action scenes in *The Matrix* (1999).

UP NEXT

This film is based on the fourth book of the Crane Iron Pentalogy, a series of five books written by the Chinese author Wang Dulu and published between 1938 and 1942. A sequel debuted simultaneously on Netflix and IMAX in early 2016.

STARRING:
Chow Yun-Fat
and
Michelle Yeoh

BOX OFFICE:
$213.5 million

DID YOU KNOW?
The world-famous cellist Yo-Yo Ma performs in the soundtrack.

SCORE BY:
Tan Dun

Saw it! ☐ Rating: ☆☆☆☆☆
Date: ___/___/_____ With: _____
Notes: _____
_____

49

LIFE IS BEAUTIFUL "LA VITA È BELLA" (ORIGINAL TITLE) ITALY

DIRECTOR:
Roberto Benigni

RELEASE DATE:
December 20, 1997
(Italy); February 12,
1999 (USA)

RATED:
PG-13
for Holocaust-
related thematic
elements

RUNTIME:
1 hour,
56 minutes

In *Life Is Beautiful*, Roberto Benigni manages to disguise the tragedies of the Holocaust with a little humor and a lot of imagination.

THE STORY

Guido Orefice (Roberto Benigni) is a happy-go-lucky Jewish storeowner with a wife and young son. Their enchanted life is uprooted when the Nazis occupy their small Italian town during World War II. The family is captured and taken to a concentration camp. Guido, a joker at heart, uses this quality to help his son, Joshua (Giorgio Cantarini), persevere through the most unbearable stages of their captivity. Guido shelters Joshua from the frightening events at the concentration camp by turning them into a big game. He promises his son that if he wins, the prize is a real tank!

Guido sets the stage for the elaborate game as soon as they arrive at the concentration camp. Instead of telling Joshua what the Nazi guard is really shouting in German, the ingenious father translates it in a much gentler way:

"The game starts now. You have to score one thousand points. If you do that, you take home a tank with a big gun. Each day we will announce the scores from that loudspeaker. The one who has the fewest points will have to wear a sign that says 'Jackass' on his back. There are three ways to lose points: One, if you cry; two, if you ask to see your mother; and three, if you're hungry and ask for a snack."

Saw it! ☐ Rating: ☆☆☆☆☆
Date: ___/___/_____ With: _____
Notes: _____
_____

CLOSE ENCOUNTERS OF THE THIRD KIND

THE STORY

Roy Neary (Richard Dreyfuss) has visions he can't explain—one is of a mountain in Wyoming he's sure he's never visited before, and he's drawn to go see it. Others experience strange things too; for example, a young boy's battery-powered toys suddenly turn on in his room. Meanwhile, scientists are mystified when they discover intact planes from a flight mission that had gone missing 30 years before. One night, Roy sees an unidentified flying object (UFO) and the bright, violent, flashing lights leave a burn mark on his face. People around the world also begin to have encounters with UFOs and report that they hear strange musical sounds—as if the UFOs are trying to communicate. Roy heads to the mountain along with the others, but the military wants to keep people away while they prepare a secret landing zone for the UFOs. Will they see aliens?

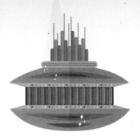

DID YOU KNOW?
Making *Close Encounters* was top secret. Costing $18 million, it was Spielberg's most expensive film at the time.

WATCH OUT FOR

Director Steven Spielberg went to great lengths to protect the film from being spoiled by early leaks of the spectacular ending. Spielberg consulted experts about the reported UFO sightings that have taken place around the world, and used that information to create a believable outcome for *Close Encounters*.

DIRECTOR:
Steven Spielberg

RELEASE DATE:
December 25, 1977

RATED:
PG
for some intense sci-fi action, mild language, and thematic elements

RUNTIME:
2 hour, 17 minutes

Saw it! ☐ Rating: ☆☆☆☆☆

Date: ___/___/_____ With: _____

Notes: _____

_____

51

STAR WARS

DIRECTOR:
George Lucas

**RELEASE
DATE:**
May 25, 1977

RATED:
PG
for sci-fi violence
and brief mild
language

RUNTIME:
2 hours,
1 minute

THE STORY

Star Wars tells the story of Luke Skywalker, Han Solo, Obi-Wan Kenobi, and Princess Leia, who together lead the Rebel Alliance against Darth Vader and the evil Empire. After Obi-Wan teaches Luke about the "Force," an invisible power that only true Jedi knights can control, the space cowboys, along with the princess and two amusing droids, R2-D2 and C-3PO, plot to destroy the Death Star space station.

WHY IT'S FAMOUS

This film was considered ahead of its time, and it has survived the test of time. *Star Wars* was later re-titled *Star Wars Episode IV A New Hope*, but any self-respecting fan refers to it simply by its birth name. Besides introducing us to some out-of-this-world characters,

"A long time ago, in a galaxy far, far away..."

galaxies, spaceships, and lightsabers, *Star Wars* pioneered a new special-effects industry. George Lucas wrote and directed the film. He also established a new company called Industrial Light & Magic (ILM) to accommodate the groundbreaking computer-generated visual effects he created for the movie. In 2012, The Walt Disney Company bought ILM as part of the $4 billion Lucasfilm deal.

Luke Skywalker and the rest of the rebels made two more films, *The Empire Strikes Back* (1980) and *Return of the Jedi* (1983). Together these three films (which you can binge-watch in one session if you are a true fan!) are known as the Star Wars Trilogy.

UP NEXT

Decades later, the obsession with *Star Wars* continues. A prequel trilogy was released between 1999–2005, including the films *The Phantom Menace, Attack of the Clones,* and *Revenge of the Sith. Star Wars: Episode VII,* the next installment, hit theaters in December 2015, and featured original *Star Wars* cast members Mark Hamill as Luke Skywalker, Harrison Ford as Han Solo, and Carrie Fisher as Princess Leia.

Disney plans to complete the third trilogy as well as release a string of spin-off films spotlighting various characters, meaning there will be new Star Wars movies for years to come!

DID YOU KNOW?

This film influenced our popular culture in so many ways that *Star Wars* is now part of the National Film Registry at the Library of Congress for being "culturally, historically, and aesthetically significant."

BOX OFFICE:
$775.3 million

MUSIC:
John Williams

SCREEN-PLAY WRITTEN BY:
George Lucas

Saw it! ☐ Rating: ☆☆☆☆☆

Date: ___/___/_____ With: _____

Notes: _____

_____

52

RAIDERS OF THE LOST ARK

DIRECTOR:
Steven
Spielberg

**RELEASE
DATE:**
June 12, 1981

RATED:

PG

for intense
sequences of
violence, graphic
images, brief
language and
sensuality

RUNTIME:
1 hour,
55 minutes

Indyyy! Iiinnndddyyy! That's short for Indiana Jones. The demanding tone heard in this hero's nickname means someone is in trouble and needs his help. Though Dr. Jones doesn't always have a rescue plan in mind, you can count on this whip-smart professor to make one up on the fly, nearly every time.

THE STORY

Harrison Ford plays the role of Dr. Indiana Jones in *Raiders of the Lost Ark*. Set in the 1930s, the U.S. government hires Jones to spoil a Nazi plan to dig up the famous biblical artifact, the Ark of the Covenant.

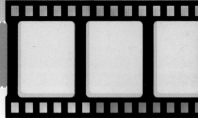

According to legend, whoever finds the Ark will possess infinite power, and Adolf Hitler wants to use it to create the most powerful army in the world. Professor Jones's knowledge of archeology and antiquities helps him determine the essential missing clue that points to the location of the Ark. From the jungles of Peru to the snowy mountains of Nepal to the hot sands of Egypt, we follow Indy on his quest to find the Ark before the enemy.

In a way, Indiana Jones was the 1980s version of a superhero. However, his outfit of choice was a pair of pants, shirt, leather jacket, hat (which he never lost!), and bullwhip. Jones was able to dash into a dangerous situation and save the day without having to change into tights or wear a cape!

UP NEXT

Raiders of the Lost Ark was so popular it led to three more films: *Indiana Jones and the Temple of Doom* (1984), *Indiana Jones and the Last Crusade* (1989), and *Indiana Jones and the Kingdom of the Crystal Skull* (2008). *Raiders of the Lost Ark* also inspired the television series, *The Young Indiana Jones Chronicles* (1992–1993), which were followed by a series of made-for-TV films that were produced from 1994–1996.

DID YOU KNOW?

Indiana Jones has inspired over a dozen video games! The popularity of this film also inspired rides and live shows at Disney theme parks in the United States, France, and Japan.

MUSIC:
John Williams

BOX OFFICE:
$389.9 million

SCREEN-PLAY WRITTEN BY:
Lawrence Kasdan

Saw it! ☐ Rating: ☆☆☆☆☆
Date: ___ / ___ / _____ With: _____
Notes: _____
_____

53

GHOSTBUSTERS

DIRECTOR:
Ivan Reitman

RELEASE DATE:
June 8, 1984

RATED:
PG
for some language, suggestive humor, frightening images

RUNTIME:
1 hour,
45 minutes

THE STORY

A trio of unemployed university parapsychologists (investigators of paranormal and psychic phenomena) establish a business to investigate and exterminate ghosts. They invent sophisticated equipment to trap spirits and work out of a neglected fire station in New York City. The highly intelligent scientists are hired to catch a ghost, and after trapping their first goblin, the Ghostbusters find themselves in high demand all over the city. Drs. Venkman (Bill Murray), Stantz (Dan Aykroyd), and Spengler (Harold Ramis) get into some funny, yet frightening, situations with phantoms and monsters when the Big Apple is caught in the middle of a poltergeist outbreak!

The government discovers that the popular ghost wranglers are not disposing of their wispy catches properly—the ghosts are being held in a containment unit in the firehouse basement. Ordered by the Environmental Protection Agency to release the ghouls, they set them free, causing mayhem in Manhattan. The mayor finds that he needs to bring order to a chaotic city. So, who's he gonna call? That's right: Ghostbusters!

WHY IT'S FAMOUS

Ghostbusters gave us a few of the most memorable lines in movie history. "I ain't afraid of no ghost," is just one of the famous sayings from *Ghostbusters*. The catchy phrase is from the film's extremely successful theme song by Ray Parker Jr. The movie became a pop culture phenomenon and led to a second film, *Ghostbusters II*, released in 1989.

It's worth mentioning that even though this film is rated PG, in 1984 the PG-13 rating wasn't around. There are some very scary super-natural beings in this movie and also some inappropriate language and behaviors that may not be suitable for the PG audience of today.

STARRING:
Bill Murray, Dan Aykroyd, Harold Ramis, and Sigourney Weaver

BOX OFFICE:
$295.2 million

SCREEN-PLAY WRITTEN BY:
Dan Aykroyd, Harold Ramis, and Rick Moranis

DID YOU KNOW?
Ghostbusters is on the American Film Institute's "AFI's 100 Years...100 Laughs" list.

Saw it! ☐ Rating: ☆☆☆☆☆
Date: ___ / ___ / _____ With: _____
Notes: _____
_____

54

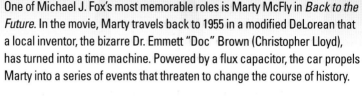

BACK TO THE FUTURE

DIRECTOR:
Robert Zemeckis

**RELEASE
DATE**:
July 3, 1985

RATED:

PG

for adult
situations/
language and
violence

RUNTIME:
1 hour,
56 minutes

One of Michael J. Fox's most memorable roles is Marty McFly in *Back to the Future*. In the movie, Marty travels back to 1955 in a modified DeLorean that a local inventor, the bizarre Dr. Emmett "Doc" Brown (Christopher Lloyd), has turned into a time machine. Powered by a flux capacitor, the car propels Marty into a series of events that threaten to change the course of history.

THE STORY

Marty finds himself 30 years in the past, in his hometown of Hill Valley, looking at the teenage versions of his mother and father. He sees his nerdy dad, George McFly (Crispin Glover), bullied by a meathead named Biff (Thomas F. Wilson).

 1 ACADEMY AWARD

"Great Scott!"

Marty tries to toughen up George so he can charm Lorraine, Marty's mother. Marty's life depends on them falling in love, after all! But instead of becoming smitten with George, Lorraine (Lea Thompson) starts liking Marty. Marty has to make sure his parents fall in love before he permanently alters time, meaning he would cease to exist in 1985—the year he came from. Harnessing 1.21 gigawatts of energy to fuel the car and return Marty to 1985 turns into the most electrifying scene of this back-in-time movie.

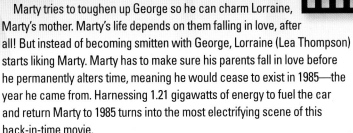

STARRING:
Michael J. Fox, Christopher Lloyd, Crispin Glover, Thomas F. Wilson, and Lea Thompson

WATCH OUT FOR

Back to the Future is an iconic 1980s movie. Its amazing success led to two more films: *Back to the Future, Part II* (1989) and *Back to the Future, Part III* (1990).

"The Power of Love" was written and performed by Huey Lewis and the News for this film. Huey Lewis has a small cameo in the movie. When Marty and his band are playing "The Power of Love" during an audition, Lewis is the judge that tells the band they are too loud!

BOX OFFICE:
$381.1 million

DID YOU KNOW?

At the end of *Back to the Future*, Doc Brown returns to Hill Valley from a trip to the future. He tells Marty to get in the DeLorean so he can take him to see the future where "we don't need roads." The date he declares he's just come from is October 21, 2015. Roads? Yes, we still need them!

MUSIC:
Alan Silvestri

Saw it! ☐ Rating: ☆☆☆☆☆
Date: ___/___/_____ With: _____
Notes: _____
_____

55

HARRY POTTER AND THE SORCERER'S STONE

DIRECTOR:
Chris Columbus

RELEASE DATE:
November 16, 2001

RATED:
PG
for some scary moments and mild language

RUNTIME:
2 hours, 32 minutes

This is the first film of eight in the Harry Potter film franchise and is based on the first of seven novels written by author and creator J.K. Rowling, who unleashed a powerful spell on the world with her magical pen.

THE STORY

Harry Potter (Daniel Radcliffe) arrived at the dreary Dursley home as a baby in a basket with a note attached. His parents, both wizards, were killed by the evil Lord Voldemort (or "He Who Must Not Be Named"), but Harry survived the attack, which left only a bolt-shaped scar on his forehead as evidence. When he is 11 years old, Harry starts getting letters of admission from Hogwarts School of Witchcraft and Wizardry, but Mr. and Mrs. Dursley, both Muggles (non-magical humans), throw them away, refusing to believe that Harry is a wizard. Rubeus Hagrid, a giant wizard, eventually delivers an acceptance letter to Harry in person. Hagrid takes Harry to Diagon Alley, a hidden wizard's marketplace. Harry buys a cape and scarf, books, ingredients for potions, and visits a shop where magic wands choose their owners. Shockingly, the wand that chooses Harry is companion to Lord Voldemort's wand— both contain a feather from the same phoenix. Harry and Hagrid then travel to Platform 9¾ in London where he boards a train to Hogwarts. On board, he meets his future best friends, Hermione Granger (Emma Watson) and Ron Weasley (Rupert Grint), who are also headed to the school. Once at Hogwarts, Harry is assigned to Gryffindor, one of the four student houses,

and becomes a member of the flying Quidditch team. Headmaster Albus Dumbledore (Richard Harris), Professor McGonagall (Maggie Smith), and Hagrid (Robbie Coltrane) know Lord Voldemort is dying and that he seeks the magic of the Sorcerer's Stone to regain his strength. Harry eventually realizes that his unfriendly potions teacher Severus Snape (Alan Rickman) is after the stone as well. Can Harry find the powerful stone before it falls into the hands of evil Lord Voldemort?

UP NEXT

The spellbinding film franchise that captivated adults and children alike includes: *Harry Potter and the Chamber of Secrets* (2002), *Harry Potter and the Prisoner of Azkaban* (2004), plus five more movies detailing the adventures of the young wizard and his friends.

WHY IT'S FAMOUS

Upon the release of the last movie in the franchise in 2011, The American Film Institute recognized the entire series with a special award, saying "The Harry Potter series marks the final triumphant chapter of a landmark series; eight films that earned the trust of a generation who wished for the beloved books of J.K. Rowling to come to life on the silver screen. The collective wizardry of an epic ensemble gave us the gift of growing older with Harry, Ron, and Hermione as the magic of Hogwarts sprung from the films and into the hearts and minds of Muggles around the world."

STARRING:
Daniel Radcliffe,
Emma Watson,
Rupert Grint,
and
Alan Rickman

BOX OFFICE:
$974.7 million

DID YOU KNOW?

If you decide to binge-watch the entire Harry Potter series, it would take you 21 hours and 49 minutes!

MUSIC:
John Williams

Saw it! ☐ Rating: ☆☆☆☆☆
Date: ___ / ___ / _____ With: _____
Notes: _____
_____

56

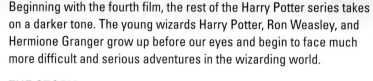

HARRY POTTER
AND THE GOBLET OF FIRE

DIRECTOR:
Mike Newell

RELEASE DATE:
November 18, 2005

RATED:
PG-13
for sequences of fantasy violence and frightening images

RUNTIME:
2 hours,
37 minutes

Beginning with the fourth film, the rest of the Harry Potter series takes on a darker tone. The young wizards Harry Potter, Ron Weasley, and Hermione Granger grow up before our eyes and begin to face much more difficult and serious adventures in the wizarding world.

THE STORY

Now 14 years old, Harry's name is the fourth spit out by the Goblet of Fire to compete in the Triwizard Tournament. Traditionally, the contest only has three representatives, each required to be 17 years old. Dumbledore can't protect Harry from the goblet's choice, which prompts the question: Who submitted Harry's name? As the tournament begins, a dark and fearsome tempest of Death Eaters ominously descends on the arena and attacks. This can only mean one thing: Voldemort (Ralph Fiennes) is back!

The attack is thwarted, and the students return to Hogwarts, where a convivial gathering of the finalists competing in the Triwizard Cup takes place. Joining Harry and Cedric Diggory (Robert Paattison) from Hogwarts are Viktor Krum (Stanislav Ianevski) from

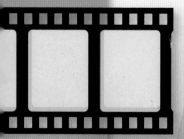

Durmstrang and Fleur Delacour (Clémence Poésy) from Beauxbatons, two neighboring schools of witchcraft and wizardry. They face each other in terror-inducing challenges involving dragons, rescuing prisoners from a dark lagoon, and finding their way out of a seemingly endless maze that holds an extra-chilling encounter for Harry. However, the fury of these tasks doesn't compare to Harry's next challenge—asking a girl to the Yule Ball.

Will Harry come face to face with his nemesis, Voldemort, and will the evil man's identity finally be revealed? Who put Harry's name in the Goblet of Fire, and why? All is revealed in this action-packed, sinister installment in the Harry Potter film series.

UP NEXT

The final four films in the Harry Potter franchise are: *Harry Potter and the Order of the Phoenix* (2007), *Harry Potter and the Half-Blood Prince* (2009), *Harry Potter and the Deathly Hallows: Part 1* (2010), and *Harry Potter and the Deathly Hallows: Part 2* (2011).

STARRING:
Daniel Radcliffe, Emma Watson, Rupert Grint, and Alan Rickman

BOX OFFICE:
$896.9 million

DID YOU KNOW?
This is the first film of the series that doesn't start out at 4 Privet Drive, the Dursley residence where Harry Potter grew up. This address and home are real. A replica of the street and its homes was built on the Warner Bros. studio lot in Leavesden, England, for filming.

MUSIC:
Patrick Doyle with main theme by John Williams

Saw it! ☐ Rating: ☆☆☆☆☆
Date: ___/___/_____ With: _____
Notes: _____
_____

57

BATMAN

DIRECTOR:
Tim Burton

RELEASE DATE:
June 23, 1989

RATED:

PG-13

for violence and gore, intense scenes, mild profanity and some sensuality

RUNTIME:
2 hours,
6 minutes

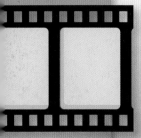

This film is considered responsible for the live-action superhero film genre so popular today. It is based on the DC Comics character Bruce Wayne, a billionaire and secret vigilante crime fighter known as Batman. In this movie, an incredible art deco Gotham City, Batcave, Batmobile, and Bat Signal all leap off the comic book pages and onto the big screen.

THE STORY

As a child, Bruce Wayne witnessed his parents' murder at the hands of a mugger and is traumatized by this event. Now an adult, Bruce lives in a mansion with his loyal butler, Alfred Pennyworth (Michael Gough), the only person who knows his double identity.

The story begins as mob boss Carl Grissom (Jack Palance) and Harvey Dent (Billy Dee Williams), the corrupt Gotham City District Attorney, plan to have their partner in crime, Jack Napier (Jack Nicholson), killed at the Axis Chemicals plant. Batman (Michael Keaton) and Commissioner James Gordon (Pat Hingle) thwart their plan, but Napier falls into a container of chemicals in the shootout and is left for dead. Years later, Bruce meets a reporter, Vicki Vale (Kim Basinger), who's looking into a vigilante helping the police and taking out criminals. At an art gallery fundraiser, a terribly disfigured man sets a trap for Vale while his cronies vandalize the artwork and scare guests. Batman arrives just in time to save the reporter, but the strange man whispers something to him that he recalls hearing from his parents' murderer. Batman realizes the man calling himself The Joker is his archenemy, and the pursuit is on.

UP NEXT

Many more Batman films and Batman series spin-off films have been made. Those that directly followed the 1989 movie include *Batman Returns* (1992), *Batman Forever* (1995), and *Batman & Robin* (1997). In 2005, Christopher Nolan directed a new Batman trilogy, including *Batman Begins* (2005), *The Dark Knight* (2008), and *The Dark Knight Rises* (2012).

DID YOU KNOW?
Prince wrote the soundtrack for *Batman* (1989).

STARRING:
Jack Nicholson, Michael Keaton, and Kim Basinger

BOX OFFICE:
$411.3 million

SCREEN-PLAY WRITTEN BY:
Sam Hamm and Warren Skaaren

Saw it! ☐ Rating: ☆☆☆☆☆

Date: ___/___/_____ With: _____

Notes: _____

_____

58

SPIDER-MAN

DIRECTOR:
Sam Raimi

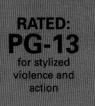

RELEASE DATE:
May 3, 2002

RATED:
PG-13
for stylized violence and action

RUNTIME:
2 hours,
1 minute

THE STORY

This film introduces us to a web-entangled high school student named Peter Parker (Tobey Maguire). While on a field trip at Oscorp Industries with his friend Harry Osborn (James Franco) and love interest Mary Jane Watson (Kirsten Dunst), Peter is bitten by a genetically engineered spider. Peter notices his vision and body starting to change and that he can suddenly produce webs from his hands! He realizes he has superhuman speed with the ability to stick to walls and climb tall buildings. Meanwhile, power-hungry Oscorp-owner Norman Osborn (Willem Dafoe)—Harry's father—wants faster progress on an experimental military drug to benefit his company, so he tests a dose of a performance vapor on himself in his lab, transforming him into the evil Green Goblin. Peter decides to use his new powers for good, and wears a costume to keep his new identity as a crime-fighting superhero a secret. Can Spider-Man save the city from the Green Goblin, keep his identity a secret, and win Mary Jane's heart in the process?

UP NEXT

Based on the Marvel Comics character by Stan Lee, *Spider-Man* has two sequels: *Spider-Man 2* (2004) and *Spider-Man 3* (2007). The franchise was re-booted with *The Amazing Spider-Man* (2012) and *The Amazing Spider-Man 2* (2014) with Andrew Garfield as Spidey. Spider-Man will also reappear in Marvel's Cinematic Universe in *Captain America: Civil War* (2016) and is slated for another stand-alone film in 2017.

Saw it! ☐ Rating: ☆☆☆☆☆
Date: ___/___/_____ With: _____
Notes: _____
_____

JURASSIC PARK

THE STORY

John Hammond (Richard Attenbor-
ough) is the rich CEO of a bioengi-
neering company who discovers how
to clone dinosaurs from fossils. He
builds Jurassic Park, a theme park
located on an isolated island off the
coast of Central America, where tourists can admire the prehistoric
animals safely behind 10,000-volt-electrified fences. However, after an
employee is killed by a Velociraptor, the park is deemed unsafe and
must be certified by experts before it is allowed to open to the public.
Hammond invites archeologists Dr. Alan Grant (Sam Neill) and Dr. Ellie
Sattler (Laura Dern), along with mathematician Dr. Ian Malcolm
(Jeff Goldblum), to tour the park and support his cause against the
government safety officials. However, the scientists are not convinced that bringing dinosaurs back to life is such a good idea. One
stormy night, an attempted employee theft shuts down the security
systems throughout the park. Things begin to go terribly wrong, and
the entire park begins to lose power, including the soaring electric
enclosures keeping the dinosaurs contained. Can the scientists and
park employees find a way to escape the island before the dinosaurs
harm anyone else?

UP NEXT

Spectacular special effects made this Michael Crichton book series
a successful film franchise. *The Lost World: Jurassic Park* (1997) and
Jurassic Park III (2001) followed the original film. *Jurassic World*
premiered in June 2015.

DIRECTOR:
Steven Spielberg

**RELEASE
DATE:**
June 11, 1993

RATED:
PG-13
for intense
science fiction
terror

RUNTIME:
2 hours,
7 minutes

Saw it! ☐ Rating: ☆☆☆☆☆

Date: ___/___/_____ With: _____

Notes: _____

_____

60

TITANIC

DIRECTOR:
James Cameron

RELEASE DATE:
December 19, 1997

RATED:

PG-13

for disaster-related peril and violence, nudity, sensuality, and brief language

RUNTIME:
3 hours,
14 minutes

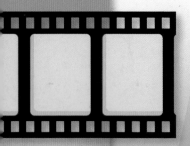

This epic story begins with actual footage shot by James Cameron of the *Titanic* sitting at the bottom of the North Atlantic Ocean. A team searches the wreckage for a rare diamond necklace that legend claims went down with the ship. They find a safe with a drawing of a woman wearing the necklace inside, and they discover that she is still alive. They invite the woman, Rose Dawson Calvert, to visit and she tells the crew what occurred on the RMS *Titanic* on April 15, 1912, the day the ship famously sank on its maiden voyage.

THE STORY

The RMS *Titanic* is the most luxurious ship ever built and leaves Southampton, England, with a score of wealthy passengers, such as Colonel John J. Astor, founder of the Astoria Hotel; Isidor Straus, founder and co-owner of Macy's; Benjamin Guggenheim, a successful businessman from Pennsylvania; and "the unsinkable" Molly Brown (Kathy Bates). Among them are first-class passengers Rose DeWitt Bukater (Kate Winslet); her fiancé, Cal Hockley (Billy Zane); and her mother, Ruth (Frances Fisher). Hockley gives Rose the Heart of the Ocean, a rare blue diamond necklace, as an engagement present.

Rose's mother is forcing her to marry Hockley for his money, and Rose feels trapped, so much so that she considers jumping off the bow of the ship! Jack Dawson (Leonardo DiCaprio), a flat-broke artist who managed to swindle his way onto third class, encounters Rose about to go overboard. He talks her out of it, and they become improbable friends from opposite social classes. Hockley sees the two and becomes suspicious of their friendship, but Rose tells him Jack saved her from falling overboard. As a reward, Rose invites Jack to dinner in first class. During the course of the voyage, Jack and Rose fall in love.

Hockley notices the pair becoming close and, out of jealousy, frames Jack for the theft of the necklace—which he plants in Jack's coat pocket—and has him handcuffed to a pipe belowdecks. Meanwhile, the ill-fated ship hits an iceberg and water pours into the hull. As women and children are evacuated, Rose jumps out of the lifeboat to find and save Jack. The re-imagined tragedy unfolds with striking detail as passengers plunge into the freezing waters, while others remain trapped in their third-class staterooms.

Can Rose and Jack hold on until help arrives? Does the team find the legendary Heart of the Ocean 85 years later?

STARRING:
Leonardo DiCaprio, Kate Winslet, Billy Zane, and Kathy Bates

BOX OFFICE:
$2.1 billion

MUSIC:
James Horner

DID YOU KNOW?

Titanic is tied with *Ben-Hur* (1959) and *The Lord of the Rings: The Return of the King* (2003) for Most Oscar Wins.

Saw it! ☐ Rating: ☆☆☆☆☆

Date: ___/___/_____ With: _____

Notes: _____

_____

61

HOW TO TRAIN YOUR DRAGON

DIRECTOR:
Dean DeBlois and
Chris Sanders

**RELEASE
DATE:**
March 26, 2010

RATED:

PG

for intense
action
sequences,
peril, and
some violence

RUNTIME:
1 hour,
38 minutes

Hiccup Horrendous Haddock III (Jay Baruchel), the son of Chief Stoick the Vast (Gerard Butler), guides us through a computer-animated Viking world where fire-breathing dragons are the perceived enemy.

THE STORY

Fire-breathing dragons have been stealing Berk's livestock and burning down its buildings for seven generations, and young Vikings are taught to slay dragons on sight. Hiccup, the Chief's scrawny and accident-prone son, is Gobber (Craig Ferguson) the blacksmith's apprentice, and he learns to use tools and make unusual inventions.

One night, Hiccup strikes down a Night Fury, the most dangerous and rare type of dragon. When he finds the small dragon and realizes he is hurt and can't fly, he doesn't have the heart to kill him. Hiccup brings the dragon food and names him Toothless because he has retractable teeth. In time, Toothless begins to trust Hiccup, and the two become friends. Hiccup learns that dragons aren't so bad after all—they only attack if they're attacked first. Hiccup makes Toothless a prosthetic fin for his tail and teaches him to fly with it. On a practice flight, Toothless takes Hiccup and his friend Astrid (America Ferrera) to the dragon's colony where a giant dragon, Red Death, feeds on smaller dragons and stolen livestock offered by the other dragons to keep it at bay. Hiccup wants to keep the location a secret, but word gets out, and the villagers mount an attack on the colony. Can Hiccup save the dragons and his village from the terrible dragon, Red Death?

UP NEXT

This clever and witty 3-D movie from DreamWorks Animation spurred two more films: *How To Train Your Dragon 2* (2014) and *How To Train Your Dragon 3,* scheduled for release in 2018.

STARRING:
Jay Baruchel, Gerard Butler, Craig Ferguson, and America Ferrera

BOX OFFICE:
$494.8 million

DID YOU KNOW?
This film is loosely based on British author Cressida Cowell's book *How to Train Your Dragon*, which is part of a 12-book children's series.

MUSIC:
John Powell

Saw it! ☐ Rating: ☆☆☆☆☆
Date: ___/___/_____ With: _____
Notes: _____
_____

62

DIRECTOR:
Peter Jackson

RELEASE DATE:
December 19, 2001

RATED:
PG-13
for epic battle sequences and some scary images

RUNTIME:
2 hours, 58 minutes

THE LORD OF THE RINGS: THE FELLOWSHIP OF THE RING

The Lord of the Rings trilogy is based on a series of books by J.R.R. Tolkien. The first of these epic fantasy films, *The Fellowship of the Ring*, introduces us to the imaginary Middle-earth and its core characters.

THE STORY

Dark Lord Sauron (Sala Baker) wants to take over Middle-earth using the almighty power of the One Ring. But the ring is taken from Sauron during a battle with Isildur. Although Sauron's body is gone, the power of the ring holds his life force, and he survives as long as the ring remains. Orcs kill the corrupt Isildur, and the ring is lost in the river Anduin until Gollum (Andy Serkis) finds it thousands of years later. Hundreds of years pass until the hobbit Bilbo Baggins (Ian Holm) takes the ring for safekeeping. Sixty years later, Bilbo gives it to his nephew, Frodo Baggins (Elijah Wood), who learns from the wizard Gandalf the Grey (Ian McKellen) that Sauron's forces will hunt him down to recover

the ring. Frodo sets off to return the ring to its birthplace at Mount Doom, the only place it can be destroyed once and for all. On the way, Frodo and his companion Samwise Gamgee (Sean Astin) avoid the Nazgûl, Sauron's soldiers, with help from Aragorn (Viggo Mortensen), who hides the pair in Rivendell. There, a meeting is called to figure out what to do with the ring—and the Fellowship is born! Together with our hobbit hero, the Fellowship travels across a vast imaginary land, encountering many obstacles, wicked creatures, and magical forces that covet the ring's power to use it for evil.

Can the Fellowship resist the ring's powerful draw, which tempts the members to use it for their own benefit? Will Frodo and the Fellowship make it to Mordor and finish their quest?

WATCH OUT FOR

The incredible detail conceived by Tolkien in his books was brought to life by Peter Jackson's extraordinary imagination. The enormity of the sets, the technical achievements, and the superb special effects will make this film trilogy transcend many generations.

The two sequels that follow are *The Two Towers* (2002) and *The Return of the King* (2003).

STARRING:
Elijah Wood, Ian McKellen, Viggo Mortensen, Cate Blanchett, Liv Tyler, and Orlando Bloom

BOX OFFICE:
$871.5 million

DID YOU KNOW?

The Return of the King won 11 Oscars, making it the film with the most awards in the trilogy, and tied with *Titanic* and *Ben-Hur* for most Oscar wins.

MUSIC:
Howard Shore

Saw it! ☐ Rating: ☆☆☆☆☆

Date: ___/___/_____ With: _____

Notes: _____

_____

63

PIRATES OF THE CARIBBEAN: THE CURSE OF THE BLACK PEARL

DIRECTOR:
Gore Verbinski

RELEASE DATE:
July 9, 2003

RATED:
PG-13
for action/
adventure
violence

RUNTIME:
2 hours,
23 minutes

An unsteady Captain Jack Sparrow (Johnny Depp) takes us across the high seas and into the world of undead pirates, cursed Aztec gold, and fierce swordfights unlike any you've ever seen in a pirate film!

THE STORY

Will Turner (Orlando Bloom) and Elizabeth Swann (Keira Knightley) have been friends since childhood, but their opposing social status hinders their union. Elizabeth saved Will as a boy from a burning ship, keeping a gold medallion necklace she took from him to prevent him from being identified as a pirate. Now a woman, Elizabeth faces a marriage proposal from the straight-laced Commodore Norrington (Jack Davenport). Distraught about the unwanted offer, she faints and falls into the bay.

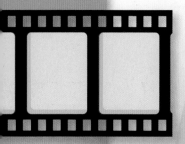

Her medallion touches the water and secretly signals the *Black Pearl* and its cursed crew to Port Royal, where they capture Elizabeth and the medallion. The coin is part of a cursed Aztec treasure, and the immortal pirates need to return all of the gold coins to the original chest to break the terrible curse. Meanwhile, Captain Jack is set on getting revenge on Captain Barbossa (Geoffrey Rush) for the mutiny and theft of his ship, the *Black Pearl*. Years ago, Barbossa betrayed Sparrow and left him stranded on an island so he could find and steal the Aztec treasure; but little did Barbossa know that the loot was cursed. Sparrow joins Will to save Elizabeth from the clutches of the rogue pirates. Can Captain Jack and Will save Elizabeth, the treasure, and return the *Black Pearl* to its rightful owner?

UP NEXT

Inspired by the Pirates of the Caribbean ride at Disneyland, this swashbuckling fantasy film starring Johnny Depp as Captain Jack Sparrow led to four sequels: *Pirates of the Caribbean: Dead Man's Chest* (2006), *Pirates of the Caribbean: At World's End* (2007), *Pirates of the Caribbean: On Stranger Tides* (2011), and *Pirates of the Caribbean: Dead Men Tell No Tales* (2017).

STARRING:
Johnny Depp,
Geoffrey Rush,
Orlando Bloom,
and Keira
Knightley

BOX OFFICE:
$654.2
million

DID YOU KNOW?

Pirates of the Caribbean is ranked among the highest-grossing film series, behind *Harry Potter, Star Wars, Batman, The Lord of the Rings, James Bond, Spider-Man, Shrek, Twilight, Transformers,* and *X-Men.*

MUSIC:
Klaus Badelt

Saw it! ☐ Rating: ☆☆☆☆☆
Date: ___/___/_____ With: _____
Notes: _____
_____

64 AVATAR

DIRECTOR:
James Cameron

RELEASE DATE:
December 18, 2009

RATED:
PG-13
for intense epic battle sequences and warfare, sensuality, language, and some smoking

RUNTIME:
2 hours, 42 minutes

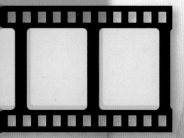

Written, directed, co-produced, and co-edited by James Cameron, this epic science-fiction film will show you the powerful vision of one of this generation's most innovative directors.

THE STORY

In the year 2154, humans have depleted Earth of its energy resources and are looking for other sources. A ship transporting people to Pandora, a distant moon as lush as a rainforest, arrives carrying civilians, scientists, and military personnel. As the ship approaches the landing site, the passengers see huge machines mining the ground for unobtanium, a mineral needed on Earth to ensure its survival.

Jake Sully (Sam Worthington), a former Marine in a wheelchair, travels six years in cryosleep to take over his scientist brother's project—Jake is a match for his deceased twin brother's Avatar, a genetically attached Na'vi and native of Pandora, who can breathe in the non-human environment.

There's an added bonus for Jake—as an Avatar he can walk again. Avatars are genetic copies of the Na'vi, controlled by their human counterparts' consciousness while they are asleep and wired to a machine that controls the slim, blue-skinned, 12-foot-tall creatures. Colonel Miles Quaritch (Stephen Lang) immediately instructs Jake and the new base residents to follow Pandora rules if they want to stay alive. They are there on a mission: They must take possession of the land where the quarry for unobtanium is located. To do this, they must convince the Na'vi to leave, or they will kill them.

The Na'vi live in harmony with nature. They've learned to tame dragon-like birds and ride them. Jake finds out the hard way that the oversized creatures of Pandora have an indiscriminant appetite, but he's saved by the gentle blue Princess Neytiri (Zoe Saldana). After getting to know the natives and understanding their way of life, Jake starts to find it very difficult to remain focused on his mission. Forced to take a stand, the future of Pandora and the Na'vi is in his hands.

UP NEXT

James Cameron is working on several *Avatar* sequels, with the next installment to come in 2017.

STARRING:
Sam Worthington, Zoe Saldana, and Sigourney Weaver

BOX OFFICE:
$2.7 billion

DID YOU KNOW?

It took 15 years for James Cameron to develop the full concept for *Avatar*. Along with the technical achievements, Cameron created the otherworldly planets, the native beings, and a new language for the Na'vi humanoids.

MUSIC:
James Horner

Saw it! ☐ Rating: ☆☆☆☆☆

Date: ___ / ___ / _____ With: _____

Notes: _____

_____

65

THE HOBBIT: AN UNEXPECTED JOURNEY

DIRECTOR:
Peter Jackson

RELEASE DATE:
December 14, 2012

RATED:
PG-13
for extended sequences of intense fantasy, action, violence and frightening images

RUNTIME:
2 hours, 49 minutes

Prodigious director Peter Jackson takes us on another fantasy adventure with three films based on J.R.R. Tolkien's novel *The Hobbit*, published in 1937.

THE STORY

Bilbo Baggins (Ian Holm) tells his nephew, Frodo Baggins (Elijah Wood), the story of his adventure 60 years earlier. Young Bilbo (Martin Freeman) is a hobbit living in the Shire who likes his orderly comfort. But his life of leisure changes overnight after the wizard Gandalf the Grey (Ian McKellen) visits him out of the blue. Gandalf proposes that Bilbo join a group of 13 dwarves (an unlucky number), led by Thorin Oakenshield (Richard Armitage), the legendary fighter and

prince of Erebor, who wants to take back the long-lost dwarven kingdom that lies beneath the Lonely Mountain. The dwarves' land is rich in gold and jewels, but it was taken from them by the dragon Smaug. Gandolf wants the nimble and compact hobbit to be the group's burglar when the need arises, but Bilbo doesn't want any part of the chaos. However, the next morning he changes his mind and decides to go on this unexpected journey with the company. Bilbo is very grumpy during the trek eastward to the Lonely Mountain—his pony is giving him bum sores. But his worries only grow as the crew is suddenly attacked by trolls, goblins, orcs, and Gollum—the creature who will change his fate in ways the hobbit can't even imagine. During his skirmish with Gollum, Bilbo sees a small ring fly out of the creature's pocket. He soon discovers that the golden band has magical powers, which he uses to escape Gollum's clutches.

The harrowing trip to the Lonely Mountain tests the dwarves, Gandolf, and Bilbo to their limits. Will the dwarves be able to reclaim their homeland? And what will Bilbo do with the One Ring?

WHY IT'S FAMOUS

The Hobbit: An Unexpected Journey, *The Desolation of Smaug* (2013), and *The Battle of the Five Armies* (2014) are considered prequels, taking place 60 years before *The Lord of The Rings* trilogy.

STARRING:
Martin Freeman,
Ian McKellen,
Ian Holm,
and Richard
Armitage

DID YOU KNOW?
The Hobbit trilogy is based on a single 300-page book. Now that's stretching the imagination!

BOX OFFICE:
$1 billion

MUSIC:
Howard Shore

Saw it! ☐ Rating: ☆☆☆☆☆
Date: ___/___/_____ With: _____
Notes: _____
_____

66

IRON MAN

DIRECTOR:
Jon Favreau

RELEASE DATE:
May 2, 2008

RATED:
PG-13
for intense sci-fi action, violence, and brief suggestive content

RUNTIME:
2 hours, 6 minutes

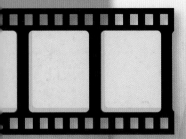

Tony Stark is Stan Lee's 1963 comic book creation and the first of the Marvel Cinematic Universe's live-action film superheroes.

THE STORY

The eccentric engineer, Tony Stark (Robert Downey Jr.), is captured by terrorists in Afghanistan after demonstrating Stark Industries' newest missile, Jericho. Stark is injured in the skirmish. Yinsen (Shaun Toub), a fellow engineer and prisoner, saves Stark by implanting a permanent electromagnet in his chest to keep the shrapnel from reaching his heart and killing him. The terrorists want

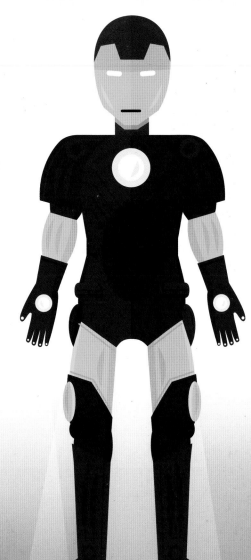

Stark to build them Jericho, and they give him the tools to do it. Stark instead builds an armored, flame-throwing suit powered by a mini arc reactor that propels him through the air, and he escapes. Meanwhile, Obadiah Stane (Jeff Bridges), his father's old business partner, plots to take over Stark Industries. He steals Tony's chest arc reactor to duplicate the Iron Man suit. Tony sends his assistant, Pepper Potts (Gwyneth Paltrow), to investigate Stane's activities, and she discovers a dark truth. Potts meets with Agent Phil Coulson (Clark Gregg) of S.H.I.E.L.D. to alert him of Stane's sinister plans.

STARRING:
Robert Downey Jr., Terrence Howard, Gwyneth Paltrow, and Jeff Bridges

WATCH OUT FOR

Watch the post-credits scene to see Nick Fury (Samuel L. Jackson) visit Tony Stark to discuss the *Avengers.* The final moments of *Iron Man* set the stage for the series of films released as part of the Marvel Cinematic Universe: *Iron Man 2* (2010), *Captain America: The First Avenger* (2011), *The Avengers* (2012), *Iron Man 3* (2013), and *Captain America: The Winter Soldier* (2014).

BOX OFFICE:
$585.1 million

DID YOU KNOW?

Iron Man director Jon Favreau wears a hairpiece and plays the role of Happy Hogan, Tony Stark's driver and loyal friend.

MUSIC:
Ramin Djawadi

Saw it! ☐ Rating: ☆☆☆☆☆

Date: ___/___/_____ With: _____

Notes: _____

_____

67

THE SOUND OF MUSIC

DIRECTOR:
Robert Wise

RELEASE DATE:
March 2, 1965

RATED:

G

General
Audiences

RUNTIME:
2 hours,
54 minutes

The Sound of Music was a 1959 Broadway musical before it became a movie in 1965. The musical was inspired by the book *The Story of the Trapp Family Singers* by Maria Augusta Trapp. This classic film turned 50 in 2015!

THE STORY

The seven von Trapp children live in Austria during World War II, amid the Nazi takeover. Their father, Austrian naval captain Georg von Trapp (Christopher Plummer), is a widower and requests a governess from Nonnberg Abbey to help with the children. The Mother Superior of the abbey asks Maria (Julie Andrews), a young and rebellious nun, to take the job. When she arrives at the stately von Trapp home, she discovers that Captain von Trapp has been disciplining the children in a militaristic style—he even uses a whistle to call them to attention! Maria steps in, and while the captain is away, she introduces the children to fun and music. As the Germans advance into Austria, the von Trapp family devises a clever plan to escape.

WHY IT'S FAMOUS

The Sound of Music won five Oscars, including one for Best Music. "Do-Re-Mi," "Sixteen Going on Seventeen," "My Favorite Things," and "So Long, Farewell" were written for the original musical, but were also included in the movie, helping make it a huge success.

STARRING:
Julie Andrews, Christopher Plummer, and Charmian Carr

BOX OFFICE:
$158.6 million (domestic)

DID YOU KNOW?
Julie Andrews was busy filming *Mary Poppins* when she was approached for the role of Maria in *The Sound of Music*.

MUSIC:
Richard Rogers and Oscar Hammerstein III

Saw it! ☐ Rating: ☆☆☆☆☆
Date: ___/___/_____ With: _____
Notes: _____

68

MARY POPPINS

DIRECTOR:
Robert Stevenson

RELEASE DATE:
August 26, 1964

RATED:
G
General Audiences

RUNTIME:
2 hours,
19 minutes

Mary Poppins is a musical film based on the 1934 fantasy book series written by P.L. Travers. It took Walt Disney 20 years to convince the author to allow Disney to turn her novel into a movie!

THE STORY

The film is set in 1910 in London, England. Mr. Banks works at a bank and is concerned with his work more than his home. Mrs. Banks is too busy trying to help women gain voting rights, and her two children, Jane (Karen Dotrice) and Michael (Matthew Garber), need someone to care for them. The family places an ad in the newspaper for a new nanny. After a strong wind blows away the line of nannies waiting for an interview, Mary Poppins (Julie Andrews) floats down from the sky and introduces herself to the Banks family. As the new nanny, she makes life

perfectly magical for the Banks children; toys and rooms are picked up at the snap of her fingers, and tea parties take place on the ceiling! With the help of her performer friend Bert (Dick Van Dyke), Mary Poppins shows the Banks children how to bring a sunny attitude and whimsical sense of adventure into everyday life.

WHY IT'S FAMOUS

The most magical part of this film is the hand-drawn animated cartoon characters that mingle and dance with real-life human actors—a cinematic feat that had not been done before! Computer animation was nowhere in sight in 1964, when Mary Poppins and her talking umbrella flew into theaters. Also, Disney animators didn't have green-screen technology to help them bring animated characters together with actors on film. Leave it to Disney to pioneer the combination of fantasy with reality in one endearing motion picture!

"Chim Chim Cher-ee" won the Oscar for Best Original Song in 1964. It is one of the many cheery songs in this five-time Academy Award-winning movie.

Mary Poppins turned 50 years old in 2014. Disney celebrated this milestone by restoring and releasing the 50th Anniversary Edition of the movie on DVD.

STARRING:
Julie Andrews, Dick Van Dyke, and David Tomlinson

BOX OFFICE:
$102.2 million (domestic)

DID YOU KNOW?

The story of how *Mary Poppins* became a movie was brought to the screen in the 2013 Disney film *Saving Mr. Banks*. And just FYI: Supercalifragilisticexpialadocious is not a real word!

MUSIC:
Richard M. Sherman and Robert B. Sherman

Saw it! ☐ Rating: ☆☆☆☆☆
Date: ___/___/_____ With: _____
Notes: _____
_____

69

WILLY WONKA & THE CHOCOLATE FACTORY

DIRECTOR:
Mel Stuart

RELEASE DATE:
June 30, 1971

RATED:
G
General Audiences

RUNTIME:
1 hour,
40 minutes

THE STORY

This story centers around Charlie (Peter Ostrom), a poor boy who passes by the eccentric, wonderful, and very mysterious Willy Wonka Chocolate Factory every day on his way home from school. The candy factory is securely locked from the outside world to guard its famous recipes. Charlie sees the other children crowd into a nearby candy shop to get a treat on their way home from school, but he can't afford one—he has to use his money to buy a loaf of bread for his family. One day, news breaks out that five lucky winners will get a private tour of the Wonka factory if they find a golden ticket hidden inside a Wonka Bar.

WHY IT'S FAMOUS

The deep lessons of this movie lie with the five golden-ticket winners. Mr. Wonka (Gene Wilder) takes it upon himself to teach these ill-raised kids a thing or two about how to behave properly.

UP NEXT

In 2005, the film was remade as *Charlie and the Chocolate Factory*, starring Johnny Depp as Willy Wonka.

DID YOU KNOW?

This classic fantasy film is based on the 1964 book *Charlie and the Chocolate Factory* by the prolific author Roald Dahl, who also wrote the screenplay.

Saw it! ☐ Rating: ☆☆☆☆☆
Date: ___ / ___ / _____ With: _____
Notes: _____
_____

ALADDIN

THE STORY

In Agrabah, the evil Jafar, advisor to the Sultan, is searching for a thief—a "Diamond in the Rough"—to go into the Cave of Wonders and retrieve a magic lamp that holds a powerful genie. Meanwhile, Princess Jasmine (Linda Larkin) is sulking because according to tradition, she must marry before her next birthday—which is in three days! But Jasmine wants to choose her own suitor and marry for love. Unhappy with her palace life, she escapes. In the marketplace, she meets Aladdin (Scott Weinger), a street rat constantly running from palace guards because he must steal to eat. The two become friends, but Aladdin and his pet monkey, Abu (Frank Welker), are arrested and thrown into the palace dungeon. Jafar convinces Aladdin to go into the Cave of Wonders to get the lamp, but the two become trapped in the cave. Aladdin rubs the lamp, and a genie appears. Genie (Robin Williams) informs Aladdin he will grant him three wishes. Aladdin's first wish is to become a prince so Jasmine will marry him. But Jafar steals the lamp and forces Genie to help him take over the city. Aladdin decides that the only way to save the kingdom is to tell Jasmine the truth about who he really is and together defeat Jafar.

DID YOU KNOW?

Robin Williams recorded over 30 hours of scripted and improvised dialogue for *Aladdin*.

DIRECTORS:
Ron Clements and John Musker

RELEASE DATE:
November 25, 1992

RATED:

G

General Audiences

RUNTIME:
1 hour, 30 minutes

Saw it! ☐ Rating: ☆☆☆☆☆
Date: ___/___/_____ With: _____
Notes: _____
_____

71

THE MUPPET MOVIE

DIRECTOR:
James Frawley

RELEASE DATE:
June 22, 1979

RATED:
G
General Audiences

RUNTIME:
1 hour, 35 minutes

THE STORY

The Muppet Movie explains how Kermit the Frog, Miss Piggy, Gonzo, Fozzie, and the rest of the Muppets meet for the first time. When a Hollywood agent (Dom DeLuise) hears Kermit singing in the swamp, he convinces him to pursue a career in show business. Kermit sets off on a cross-country road trip from Florida to California and meets the other Muppets along the way. The trip hits some speed bumps when a fast-food chain owner sees Kermit and wants him to become the mascot for the fried-frog-legs restaurant.

WHY IT'S FAMOUS

The greatest challenge for the filmmakers was making the puppets seem lifelike and walk on their own two feet for their first full feature-length movie! When Kermit pedals his bike, you don't see strings, rods, or puppeteers. Where is Jim Henson, creator of The Muppets, while Kermit sits on a log in the pond singing? Apparently, Henson was below the surface in a water-resistant contraption, where he communicated with the crew on a walkie-talkie.

   Steve Martin, Bob Hope, Mel Brooks, and Orson Welles all appear in this movie. However, the real stars are Jim Henson and the master puppeteers who magically work behind, over, and under the scenes to bring The Muppets to life!

UP NEXT

There are 12 more movies featuring The Muppets, from *The Great Muppet Caper* (1981) to *Muppets Most Wanted* (2014), which stars Tina Fey and Ricky Gervais.

Saw it! ☐ Rating: ☆☆☆☆☆
Date: ___/ ___/ _____ With: _____
Notes: _____
_____

THE LITTLE MERMAID

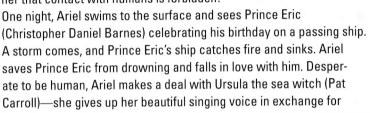

THE STORY

Disney's musical animated film introduces us to Ariel, a mermaid princess, who has everything a 16-year-old girl could wish for but still dreams of life on land. When Ariel (Jodi Benson) yearns to go above water, Sebastian (Samuel E. Wright), her crab side-kick and King Triton's trusted adviser, reminds her that contact with humans is forbidden! One night, Ariel swims to the surface and sees Prince Eric (Christopher Daniel Barnes) celebrating his birthday on a passing ship. A storm comes, and Prince Eric's ship catches fire and sinks. Ariel saves Prince Eric from drowning and falls in love with him. Desperate to be human, Ariel makes a deal with Ursula the sea witch (Pat Carroll)—she gives up her beautiful singing voice in exchange for legs. However, if the prince doesn't fall in love with her in three days, Ariel will lose her voice permanently and become Ursula's prisoner. Ariel is faced with a tough decision: is her true love worth the risk?

WHY IT'S FAMOUS

The Little Mermaid marked the beginning of the Disney Renaissance. Walt Disney Animation Studios changed the animation landscape by combining classic stories with stage musical-quality songs in a string of successful animated films.

DID YOU KNOW?

The Little Mermaid was first a fairy tale. In 1837 Danish author Hans Christian Andersen wrote a story about a mermaid who wanted to become a human.

DIRECTORS:
Ron Clements
and
John Musker

RELEASE DATE:
November 17, 1989

RATED:
G
General Audiences

RUNTIME:
1 hour,
23 minutes

Saw it! ☐ Rating: ☆☆☆☆☆

Date: ___/___/_____ With: _____

Notes: _____

_____

73

BEAUTY AND THE BEAST

DIRECTOR:
Gary Trousdale
and Kirk Wise

RELEASE DATE:
November 22, 1991

RATED:

G

General
Audiences

RUNTIME:
1 hour,
24 minutes

"A tale as old as time..."

Beauty and the Beast is a fairy tale that has been around for centuries. As Disney did with other classic stories, the animation studio adapted the traditional story into a unique Disney musical.

THE STORY

Belle (Paige O'Hara) loves reading stories about faraway places, and she secretly wishes for more than just an ordinary life. This makes her different from the other girls in town who do chores at home and don't like to read. Belle's father, Maurice (Rex Everhart), is an inventor and doesn't fit in with the rest of the town either. One day, Maurice leaves the village to enter his newest invention at a fair, and he gets lost in the woods. He stumbles upon a dark and abandoned castle. He goes inside looking for directions, but meets the angry Beast (Robby Benson), who throws him in the dungeon! Beast was once a handsome prince, but a wandering witch disguised as an ugly, old beggar woman cast a spell over him after he arrogantly denied to help her when she knocked on the castle doors. Belle goes to the castle to save her father, but when she meets the horrible Beast, she offers to take her father's place so he can go free. Can Belle save herself, her father, and break the Beast's spell?

MUSIC:
Alan Menken

BOX OFFICE:
$424.9 million

DID YOU KNOW?

Mrs. Potts (a teapot), Chip (a teacup), Lumière (a candelabrum), and Cogsworth (a clock) are new characters Disney created to transform the classic *Beauty and the Beast* tale into a timeless film.

ORIGINAL STORY BY:
Jeanne-Marie Leprince de Beaumont

Saw it! ☐ Rating: ☆☆☆☆☆
Date: ___/___/_____ With: _____
Notes: _____
_____

74

THE LION KING

DIRECTORS:
Roger Allers and
Rob Minkoff

**RELEASE
DATE**:
June 24, 1994

RATED:
G
General
Audiences

RUNTIME:
1 hour,
29 minutes

THE STORY

The Lion King is a completely original story and centers on Simba, an overconfident lion cub next in line to become king of the Pride Lands in the African savanna. His jealous uncle, Scar (Jeremy Irons), tricks Simba into thinking he caused his father Mufasa's (James Earl Jones) death. Scar tells him that the other lions will blame Simba and leaving is the only way he can save himself. Overwhelmed with shame, little Simba (Jonathan Taylor Thomas) runs into the desert, and Scar takes over as king. Simba meets Timon (Nathan Lane), a meerkat, and Pumbaa (Ernie Sabella), a warthog, and they become an irresistible trio of friends. Timon and Pumbaa's motto for living in the jungle is "Hakuna Matata," a Swahili phrase that means "no worries." Is it because they only have to worry about what their next meal will be? Simba (Matthew Broderick) grows up, and returns with his childhood friend Nala to the Pride Lands to reclaim his proper place as king.

The Academy Award winning music, including Elton John's "The Circle of Life" and "Can You Feel the Love Tonight," is ingrained in the Millennial generation like a historical event.

DID YOU KNOW?
After 57 years and 54 films, Pumbaa is the first character to fart in a Disney movie.

UP NEXT

In addition to two home entertainment sequels, *The Lion King* also became a successful stage musical.

Saw it! ☐ Rating: ☆☆☆☆☆

Date: ___/___/_____ With: _____

Notes: _____

_____

THE PRINCESS AND THE FROG

THE STORY

Tiana dreams of opening an elegant restaurant in New Orleans where she can serve her father's special gumbo and sweet beignets. Her rich friend Charlotte dreams of marrying a handsome prince. Tiana's father tells her that wishing for something is just the start; she needs to work hard to make her dreams come true.

Prince Naveen, a broke, fun-loving royal from Maldonia, travels to New Orleans looking for a rich Southern belle to marry. Charlotte's father, Big Daddy La Bouff (John Goodman), hosts a masquerade ball in honor of the prince. Earlier that day, Naveen meets Dr. Facilier (Keith David), an evil witch doctor who promises to make all his dreams come true. Dr. Facilier's voodoo spell turns the prince into a frog and disguises his valet as the prince! At Charlotte's ball, Tiana is dressed as a princess, and Naveen convinces her to kiss him to break the spell. Instead of reversing the spell, Tiana turns into a frog too!

WHY IT'S FAMOUS

After 72 years, *The Princess and the Frog* introduced Disney's first-ever African-American princess.

DIRECTORS:
Ron Clements and John Musker

RELEASE DATE:
December 11, 2009

RATED:
G
General Audiences

DID YOU KNOW?

Grammy winner Alicia Keys auditioned three times for the part of Tiana, but she ultimately lost to Tony Award-winner Anika Noni Rose.

RUNTIME:
1 hour, 37 minutes

Saw it! ☐ Rating: ☆☆☆☆☆
Date: ___/___/_____ With: _____
Notes: _____

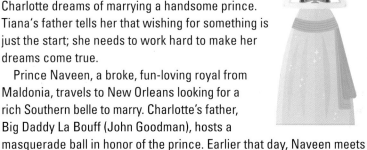

76

FROZEN

DIRECTORS:
Chris Buck and
Jennifer Lee

RELEASE DATE:
November 27, 2013

RATED:

G

for some action
and mild rude
humor

RUNTIME:
1 hour,
42 minutes

This musical fantasy was inspired by *The Snow Queen*, the 1844 fairy tale written by Hans Christian Andersen. *Frozen* beat records for Disney and the film industry as a whole, becoming the highest-grossing animated film of all time.

THE STORY

Princess Elsa (Idina Menzel) has a strange, magical gift that allows her to create ice and snow at will—and sometimes by accident too. As a little girl, Elsa was playing with her sister Anna (Kristen Bell), when she accidentally let a blast of cold knock Anna unconscious. Her parents, the King and Queen of Arendelle, sought help from a magical troll, who erased Anna's memories of Elsa's magical powers and restored her health. From that day onward, Elsa stayed hidden within the castle to keep from hurting Anna or revealing her powers to anyone else. Many years go by and Elsa and Anna's parents are killed in a shipwreck. The sisters, once close, are now distant.

Elsa turns 21 and is now of age to take the throne. Since she hasn't been seen in years, the city is bursting with excitement in preparation for her coronation. No one is more anxious to see Elsa than her younger sister Anna. At the coronation, Anna meets Prince Hans and they quickly bond. Meanwhile, Elsa is frightened she won't be able to control her emotions, which may unleash the blasts that freeze anything they touch. Nevertheless, the grand occasion goes on without any problems, until Hans proposes to Anna at the reception. They ask for the queen's blessing to marry, but Elsa refuses and is suspicious of the sudden union. The siblings fight, and Elsa has an icy emotional outburst that releases a volley of sharp icicles across the ballroom! Devastated and afraid, Elsa runs away, leaving a snowy wake in her path. But Anna refuses to let her sister run away. With help from Kristoff (Jonathan Groff), a rough mountain man; his sidekick Sven, a reindeer; and a talking snowman, Olaf (Josh Gad), they set off to bring Elsa back. When they find her, Elsa becomes angry and orders them to leave. Anna resists, and Elsa accidentally strikes her again and freezes her heart. Only an "act of true love" can keep Anna's heart from freezing solid forever. Who will save Anna? Will Elsa return to Arendelle to thaw the city and rule over her kingdom?

STARRING:
Kristen Bell,
Idina Menzel,
Jonathan Groff,
Alan Tudyk, and
Josh Gad

BOX OFFICE:
$1.2 billion

MUSIC:
Kristen Anderson-Lopez
and
Robert Lopez

DID YOU KNOW?
This is the first time the bond of sisterly love is the focus of a Disney film rather than the traditional prince-and-princess happily-ever-after ending.

Saw it! ☐ Rating: ☆☆☆☆☆
Date: ___/___/_____ With: _____
Notes: _____
_____

77

THE WIZARD OF OZ

DIRECTOR:
Victor Fleming

RELEASE DATE:
August 25, 1939

RATED:
G
General Audiences

RUNTIME:
1 hour,
42 minutes

The Wizard of Oz is arguably the most popular film ever! The original movie is based on the book, *The Wonderful Wizard of Oz*, written by L. Frank Baum and published in 1899.

THE STORY

After Dorothy and her little dog Toto are swept up by a tornado, they are magically transported to the Land of Oz. There, Dorothy meets Glinda (Billie Burke) the good witch and learns that only the Wizard of Oz can send her home to Kansas. On her way to see the Wizard, she stumbles across three characters also in need of the Wizard's help. The tale of this unlikely group of friends who overcome obstacles in search of the Wizard is timeless, and the lessons we learn from this film are still relevant today.

We all need courage to persevere, and like the Cowardly Lion (Bert Lahr), if we're afraid to do something and we don't try, we'll never know if we are capable of doing it. While poor Scarecrow (Ray Bolger)thinks he isn't intelligent, he is able to think on his feet when needed. And caring for one another is what friends do—just ask the Tin Man (Jack Haley).

WHY IT'S FAMOUS

One of the most important messages in *The Wizard of Oz* is simple: "There's no place like home." Growing up, we sometimes think our friends have it so much better than we do. Hopefully, we don't have to travel all the way to Oz to understand that the yellow brick road leads right to the people who love us most: our family.

This film is also a classic "because, because, because" of the wonderful songs and script lines that have become part of our daily language. The famous line "Lions and tigers and bears, oh my!" is chanted by Dorothy, Tin Man, Scarecrow, and Cowardly Lion as they walk through the bewitched forest on their way to the Emerald City in search of the great and powerful Wizard of Oz.

Watch *The Wizard of Oz* and see how many songs, classic lines, and examples of human virtues you recognize!

STARRING:
Judy Garland, Ray Bolger, Bert Lahr, and Jack Haley

BOX OFFICE:
$23.3 million

MUSIC:
Harold Arlen

DID YOU KNOW?

The ruby slippers worn by Dorothy in the film are on permanent display at the Smithsonian museum in Washington, D.C. In 2014, the suit worn by the Cowardly Lion sold at auction for $3.1 million.

Saw it! ☐ Rating: ☆☆☆☆☆

Date: ___/___/_____ With: _____

Notes: _____

_____

SPACE JAM

DIRECTOR:
Joe Pytka

RELEASE DATE:
November 15, 1996

RATED:
PG
for some mild cartoon language

RUNTIME:
1 hour, 28 minutes

WHY IT'S FAMOUS

Warner Bros. produced its first technically-enhanced movie with *Space Jam,* which features classic Looney Tunes cartoon characters mixed with live action stars Michael Jordan, Bill Murray, Larry Bird, Charles Barkley, and Patrick Ewing.

THE STORY

A young Michael Jordan is shooting hoops with his dad and dreams about playing with the NBA. Fast-forward to Jordan on the baseball field trying to conquer another sport. Later, on the golf course, Jordan is suddenly sucked down a hole into Looney Tunes Land.

Meanwhile, in the cartoon world, Swackhammer (Danny DeVito) is the owner of Moron Mountain, an amusement park planet in peril of being foreclosed. He sends the Nerdlucks, five tiny aliens with big weapons, to kidnap Bugs Bunny and company for a new attraction. Bugs makes a deal to play basketball with them: if they win, they get their freedom. The Nerdlucks harness the talents of star NBA basketball players and become the Monstars, but Bugs, Daffy, Porky Pig, Tweety, and the rest of the Looney Tunes gang are only able to capture Jordan. Let the game begin!

DID YOU KNOW?

The song "I Believe I Can Fly," featured in *Space Jam* and written by R. Kelly, won the Grammy for Best Song Written Specifically for a Motion Picture or for Television.

Saw it! ☐ Rating: ☆☆☆☆☆

Date: ___/___/_____ With: _____

Notes: _____

_____

COOL RUNNINGS

THE STORY

A Jamaican Olympic athlete hopeful, Derice Bannock (Leon), doesn't qualify for the 100-meter event at the trials because his fellow runner, Junior Bevil (Rawle D. Lewis), trips and falls, causing Derice and a few other runners to hit the ground as well. With his dreams for an Olympic run shattered, Derice asks competition organizer Coolidge (Winston Stona) for a second chance, but he's denied. Looking at an old photo in Coolidge's office, Derice asks who the stranger standing next to his gold medal-winning father is. Irving Blitzer (John Candy) was an Olympic bobsled medalist, but he had his medals stripped after he was caught cheating. Derice realizes he can still become an Olympic athlete—as a bobsledder! He contacts Irv about putting together a Jamaican bobsled team to compete in the Winter Olympics in Calgary, Canada. This makes no sense to the others, but Derice and Irv try to recruit for the team, and they end up with Sanka Coffie (Doug E. Doug), Junior Bevil, and Yul Brenner (Malik Yoba).

DID YOU KNOW?

Disney's sports comedy film about the 1988 Olympic bobsled team from Jamaica is loosely based on a true story.

DIRECTOR:
Jon Turteltaub

RELEASE DATE:
October 1, 1993

RATED:

PG

for mild language and brief violence

RUNTIME:
1 hour, 38 minutes

Saw it! ☐ Rating: ☆☆☆☆☆

Date: ___/___/_____ With: _____

Notes: _____

_____

80

THE KARATE KID

DIRECTOR:
John G. Avildsen

**RELEASE
DATE:**
June 22, 1984

RATED:
PG
for adult
situations/
language,
violence

RUNTIME:
2 hours,
6 minutes

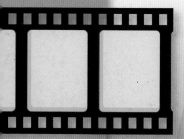

THE STORY

Daniel LaRusso (Ralph Macchio) moves from New Jersey to Los Angeles with his mother. In a new city and new high school, the mild-mannered teenager faces a group of bullies who study karate at the Cobra Kai Dojo. The sensei at Cobra Kai teaches his pupils a vicious form of karate. After getting beat up regularly by Johnny Lawrence (William Zabka) and his group of thugs for dating Johnny's ex-girlfriend, Ali Mills (Elisabeth Shue), Daniel decides it's time to take matters into his own hands.

Mr. Miyagi (Pat Morita), the janitor at Daniel's apartment complex, seems like a peculiar old man at first—he catches flies with chopsticks! He shocks Daniel one day when he intervenes and single-handedly defeats Daniel's teenage attackers, revealing his superior karate skills. Daniel asks the handyman to teach him to fight. Miyagi refuses and instead offers to

go with Daniel to the Cobra Kai Dojo and show him how to resolve the conflict peacefully. However, sensei Kreese (Martin Kove), scoffs at their peaceful offer. After seeing this, the wise old man agrees to teach Daniel how to defend himself so he can face Johnny at the All-Valley Karate Tournament using a different method of martial arts, one that requires a balance of mind and spirit. The process is slow and involves boring tasks that Miyagi considers essential for muscle memory. "Wax on, use the left. Wax off, use the right," he tells a frustrated Daniel while he makes him clean his car. Daniel wants to quit and thinks Miyagi is just using him to do his chores. As the lessons continue, Daniel starts to understand how he can apply the principles he's learned to his daily life—especially with Ali.

At the tournament, Daniel surprises everyone and makes it to the semi-finals. But one of Kreese's students knocks Daniel out of the competition with an illegal kick to the knee. Johnny is practically declared the winner, except that Daniel has one more surprise under his belt. Will Daniel's bullies finally learn to respect him?

UP NEXT
Also see *The Karate Kid, Part II* (1986) and *The Karate Kid, Part III* (1989). A remake of *The Karate Kid* starring Jaden Smith was released in 2010.

STARRING:
Ralph Macchio, William Zabka, Elizabeth Shue, Pat Morita, and Martin Kove

BOX OFFICE:
$90.8 million (domestic)

SCREEN-PLAY WRITTEN BY:
Robert Mark Kamen

DID YOU KNOW?
The director of *The Karate Kid* also directed *Rocky* (1976).

Saw it! ☐ Rating: ☆☆☆☆☆

Date: ___/___/_____ With: _____

Notes: _____

_____

RUDY

DIRECTOR:
David Anspaugh

RELEASE DATE:
October 22, 1993

RATED:
PG
for mild language

RUNTIME:
1 hour, 54 minute

This inspirational sports film is based on a true story about the life of Daniel "Rudy" Ruettiger, who played football at the University of Notre Dame in 1975.

THE STORY

Rudy (Sean Astin) refuses to accept what everyone tells him about his college prospects: He has neither the grades nor the athletic build to play for the Fighting Irish. But this doesn't stop him from following his dream. After graduating from high school, Rudy and his best friend Pete (Christopher Reed) work at a steel mill. A tragic accident kills Pete, the only one who encouraged Rudy's dream. Against his family's will, Rudy leaves for South Bend, Indiana. He enrolls at Holy Cross Junior College across the way from Notre Dame and improves his grades with help from D-Bob (Jon Favreau), a tutor who discovers that Rudy is dyslexic. After working hard for two years, he applies and is accepted to Notre Dame. Now all he has to do is get on the football team as a walk-on. Rudy sleeps in the groundskeeper's office on a cot and is allowed to practice with the team. All he wants is to wear the uniform and play one game so his name will be on the team's roster. This is a tall order considering he is "5-foot nothin'" and weighs "a hundred and nothing."

DID YOU KNOW?
In 2006, *Rudy* was ranked the 54th-most inspiring film of all time in the American Film Institute's "AFI's 100 Years...100 Cheers" series.

Saw it! ☐ Rating: ☆☆☆☆☆
Date: ___ / ___ / _____ With: _____
Notes: _____
_____

CHARIOTS OF FIRE

This British historical drama is based on the true story of two Olympic runners, Eric Liddell (Ian Charleson) and Harold Abrahams (Ben Cross), who competed in the 1924 games in Paris.

THE STORY

In a flashback from Harold Abrahams's memorial service, we're taken to his first day at Cambridge University as a privileged English-Jewish student just after World War I. Showing off, Abrahams impresses everyone by accomplishing the Trinity Great Court Run, completing a lap around the quad in the time it takes for the clock to strike the noon bells. Liddell is a Christian, born of Scottish missionaries in China. They both have the gift of speed, but also have something to prove—their worth to society and to themselves. Their personalities clash, but on the track they both focus on winning and earn spots on the British Olympic team. However, they both face obstacles, too. How these young men resolve their issues and then go on to leave an indelible impression on British history is a lesson worth taking to heart.

DIRECTOR:
Hugh Hudson

RELEASE DATE:
March 30, 1981 (UK); April 9, 1982 (USA)

DID YOU KNOW?

Eric Liddell went back to do missionary work in China. He died under Japanese captivity after they invaded China. He passed away a few months before liberation in 1945.

RATED:
PG
for adult situations/ language

RUNTIME:
1 hour, 59 minutes

Saw it! ☐ Rating: ☆☆☆☆☆
Date: ___/___/_____ With: _____
Notes: _____
_____

FIELD OF DREAMS

DIRECTOR:
Phil Alden Robinson

RELEASE DATE:
May 5, 1989

RATED:
PG
for thematic elements and some language

RUNTIME:
1 hour, 47 minutes

THE STORY

Ray Kinsella (Kevin Costner) trades his city life for a quiet farm in Iowa. One day, he hears a voice say, "If you build it, he will come." He hears the voice several more times and suddenly understands what it's telling him. He needs to build a baseball field on his land. His wife Annie (Amy Madigan), is skeptical about this harebrained idea, but she supports her husband.

Ray follows his dream and bulldozes the cornstalks to make way for a baseball diamond. After the work is finished, Ray sees an old-time uniformed baseball player come out of the cornfield and onto the field. It's Shoeless Joe Jackson (Ray Liotta). Ray searches out author Terence Mann (James Earl Jones) and an older doctor, Moonlight Graham (Burt Lancaster), who also played baseball, and takes them back to the farm to join the rest of the ghosts on the field.

Everyone thinks he's crazy, and Ray starts to doubt himself. Then something magical happens out on the field that convinces everyone that pursuing a dream is sometimes worth the risks.

DID YOU KNOW?

The Chicago White Sox scandal of 1919 is a true event. Accused of throwing games against the Cincinnati Reds to fix the World Series, the team was banned for life from baseball.

Saw it! ☐ Rating: ☆☆☆☆☆

Date: ___/___/_____ With: _____

Notes: _____

_____

REMEMBER THE TITANS

THE STORY

In this adaptation of a true story from 1971, Coach Boone (Denzel Washington) is placed at T.C. Williams High School after the school board adopts the state's integration plan. Coach Bill Yoast (Will Patton), a white man, is demoted to assistant coach to make room for the new system; a black coach is needed to coach the newly integrated football team. Yoast feels humiliated and wants to quit, but the white players also threaten to quit, so he swallows his pride and stays on. Boone is threatened by the administration—if he loses a single game, he'll be fired! Resistance to desegregation is evident in the racial tensions among the players, who train exceptionally hard because there is so much riding on their first season as a team. The monumental task of bringing this new team together to win is now on Boone's shoulders. Can he do it?

DIRECTOR:
Boaz Yakin

RELEASE DATE:
September 29, 2000

DID YOU KNOW?

The scene where a brick flies through Coach Boone's window is partially true. It wasn't a brick, but a toilet seat that was flung at his window.

RATED:

PG

for thematic elements and some language

WHY IT'S FAMOUS

This movie brings us to the edge of our seats as we see how racial prejudice melts away, and the newly formed bond among the players results in a history-making season.

RUNTIME:
1 hour, 53 minutes

Saw it! ☐ Rating: ☆☆☆☆☆
Date: ___ / ___ / _____ With: _____
Notes: _____
_____

85

SEABISCUIT

DIRECTOR:
Gary Ross

RELEASE DATE:
July 25, 2003

RATED:
PG-13
for some sexual
situations and
violent sports-
related images

RUNTIME:
2 hours,
20 minutes

This beautiful biographical film is based on the 2001 best-selling novel by Laura Hillenbrand.

THE STORY

Red Pollard (Tobey Maguire) is abandoned by his parents during the Great Depression. He grows up with a horse owner who uses him to maintain his stables and, angry with his lot in life, takes his frustrations out in boxing matches. He gets injured and ends up blind in one eye. Charles Howard (Jeff Bridges) is a self-made wealthy man who becomes a stable owner. He meets Tom Smith (Chris Cooper), an eccentric horse trainer with a knack for training reluctant horses. Charles hires Tom to find him a horse and train it to win. He chooses Seabiscuit, a small, lazy, stubborn horse with racehorse pedigree. Now they need a jockey. Although Red understands Seabiscuit, he's too tall for a jockey. The three men work together to produce a race-worthy horse that, against all odds, goes on to race War Admiral, a Triple Crown winner. In the process, Seabiscuit becomes a hero for the heartbroken in 1930s America with his inspiring story.

DID YOU KNOW?
The Triple Crown of Thoroughbred Racing is the most coveted title and consists of winning three races: the Kentucky Derby, the Preakness Stakes, and the Belmont Stakes.

Saw it! ☐ Rating: ☆☆☆☆☆
Date: ___/___/_____ With: _____
Notes: _____

A LEAGUE OF THEIR OWN

This movie is a fictionalized version of the origins and development of the All-American Girls Professional Baseball League (AAGPBL).

THE STORY

In 1943, when most of the men were called to fight during World War II, Major League Baseball was on the verge of shutting down. Team owners got together to find a solution, and Walter Harvey (Gary Marshall), candy magnate and owner of the Chicago Cubs, persuaded them to finance a women's league. Jimmy Dugan (Tom Hanks), a former Cubs player, is recruited to coach one of the new all-girl teams. Ball player Dottie Hinson (Geena Davis) and her sister Kit Keller (Lori Petty) are brought from Oregon to Chicago for the tryouts. There ends up being four teams: the Rockford Peaches, Racine Belles, Kenosha Comets, and the South Bend Blue Sox.

WHY IT'S FAMOUS

The women played baseball while their husbands were away at war, and nobody thought the league would amount to much— but it did. And how the players managed to overcome the barriers women face in sports both then and now is the very heart of this story.

DID YOU KNOW?

The AAGPBL survived even after the men returned from the war. The women continued to play baseball until 1954. *A League of Their Own* was selected for preservation in the United States National Film Registry in 2012.

DIRECTOR:
Penny Marshall

RELEASE DATE:
July 1, 1992

RATED:
PG
for language

RUNTIME:
2 hours,
8 minutes

Saw it! ☐ Rating: ☆☆☆☆☆
Date: ___/___/_____ With: _____
Notes: _____
_____

87 MIRACLE

DIRECTOR:
Gavin O'Connor

RELEASE DATE:
February 6, 2004

RATED:
PG
for language and some rough sports action

RUNTIME:
2 hours, 15 minutes

WHY IT'S FAMOUS

The 1980 Winter Olympic Games were held in Lake Placid, New York. *Miracle* recounts the true story about how the underdog United States hockey team's coach Herb Brooks was selected, how the Olympic team was formed, and what it took for the men's hockey team to make it to the medal round against the Soviets in the 1980 Winter Olympic Games.

THE STORY

Herb Brooks (Kurt Russell) is a former Olympian and the University of Minnesota's head coach. He interviews with the U.S. Olympic Committee (USOC) to be the hockey team's coach and proposes his own training program for the men. The team would be facing the Soviets, who were a force in the sport. Coach Brooks does something unorthodox; he picks 26 players, regardless of the tryouts held in Colorado Springs, and disregards the USOC's recommendations. College rivalries heat up during the intense practices, but Brooks puts an end to the arguments with a rigorous practice routine. Eventually the team starts racking up the wins, leading to the gold medal rounds against the heavy favorites: the Soviet and the Finnish teams. Do they win gold?

DID YOU KNOW?
"Herbies" are named after Coach Herb Brooks. These punishing wind sprints were his preferred drill!

Saw it! ☐ Rating: ☆☆☆☆☆
Date: ___/___/_____ With: _____
Notes: _____
_____

BEND IT LIKE BECKHAM

THE STORY

In this fictional comedy drama, Jesminder "Jess" Bhamra (Parminder Nagra) is the 18-year-old daughter of traditional Punjabi parents living in the suburbs of London. Jess's parents only expect two things from her: to learn to cook a traditional Indian meal and to marry an Indian boy. However, Jess is obsessed with playing soccer, a sport that respectable Indian girls don't play. Jess resorts to hiding her love of soccer from her parents since they have banned her from playing. Kicking the ball around with the boys at the park one day, Juliette Paxton (Keira Knightley) notices Jess's impressive skills and recruits her to play with the Hounslow Harriers, a local women's team. Jess joins the team and develops a crush on Joe, the team's coach. That would be all right except Joe is Irish, and he can't date his players. Also, Juliette likes him too. Complicated? You bet!

Jess continues to play soccer with one goal in mind: to get a scholarship to attend the prestigious Santa Clara University in California. Can her parents' old traditions coexist with Jess's new ones?

DID YOU KNOW?

Parminder Nagra wasn't a soccer player. She went to boot camp to learn a tough Brazilian method that teaches flashy moves. After a private screening of this film, David Beckham told the actress she did a good job.

DIRECTOR:
Gurinder Chadha

RELEASE DATE:
April 12, 2002 (UK);
August 1, 2003 (USA)

RATED:
PG-13
for language and sexual content

RUNTIME:
1 hour, 52 minutes

Saw it! ☐ Rating: ☆☆☆☆☆

Date: ___/___/_____ With: _____

Notes: _____

_____

89

THE SANDLOT

DIRECTOR:
David M. Evans

RELEASE DATE:
April 7, 1993

RATED:

PG

for some language and kids chewing tobacco

RUNTIME:
1 hour,
41 minutes

THE STORY

This is not a typical sports film about kids becoming so good at baseball that they beat all the other teams. In fact, no other teams play in *The Sandlot*.

In the summer of 1960, Scotty Smalls (Tom Guiry) and his just-remarried mother move to a new town near Los Angeles. The adolescent finds new friends at the local sandlot, where eight players need a ninth man to complete the team. Perfect, right? Wrong. Smalls can't play baseball to save his life. He's so bad at sports, he doesn't even know who Babe Ruth is (he thought he was a girl!). To fit in with the team, he asks his stepdad (Denis Leary) to teach him to throw and catch. His stepdad is an avid baseball fan who collects priceless memorabilia, but they never find the time to play. Benny "The Jet" Rodriguez (Mike Vitar) is the best player on the neighborhood team and takes Smalls under his wing. He teaches him what he needs to know about baseball and gets him a spot on the team.

During a particularly hot and dusty day, the boys join in on other summertime rituals, like going to the local pool and challenging each other to kiss the cute lifeguard, Wendy Peffercorn (Marley Shelton). Though they try to fool her into kissing one of them, they end up getting kicked out of the pool. Back at the sandlot, the boys are playing ball, and they accidentally hit their only ball behind the fence where a huge and vicious dog they call "The Beast" lives. They are all too scared to get it back, but Smalls sees his chance to be a hero. He runs home to his stepdad's office, grabs a ball—which is signed by Babe Ruth—out of its case, and runs back to the field to save the day! Except that this ball also goes flying over the fence. They have to retrieve *that* ball. But how will they get around The Beast?

UP NEXT

This cherished coming-of-age movie inspired two more: *The Sandlot 2* (2005) and *The Sandlot 3* (2007).

STARRING:
Tom Guiry,
Denis Leary,
Mike Vitar, and
Patrick Renna

BOX OFFICE:
$33.8 million

DID YOU KNOW?

If you don't know what PF Flyers are, you will after you see the sneakers worn by Benny Rodriguez in this movie. The boys in *The Sandlot* have always been cool.

MUSIC:
David Newman

Saw it! ☐ Rating: ☆☆☆☆☆
Date: ___/___/_____ With: _____
Notes: _____
_____

90

DEAD POETS SOCIETY

1 ACADEMY AWARD

DIRECTOR:
Peter Weir

RELEASE DATE:
June 9, 1989

RATED:
PG
for language,
substance use,
and thematic
elements

RUNTIME:
2 hours,
8 minutes

THE STORY

On the first day of school at Welton Academy, Professor John Keating (Robin Williams) tells the all-boy class to call him "O Captain, My Captain!" He stands on the desks and inspires the class to *carpe diem*, meaning "seize the day!" Neil Perry (Robert Sean Leonard), Knox, Richard, Todd (Ethan Hawke), Meeks, Pitts, and Charlie take the professor's message to heart; they don't have to follow their parents' wishes nor submit to school rules. The boys resurrect the historic Dead Poets Society after they find out their teacher used to be a member of the club. The boys meet in secret and discuss what they really want for themselves, rather than what their parents expect. However, Neil is one of Welton Academy's most prized students, and his parents expect him to go to Harvard University. But Neil wants to be an actor and gets involved in a school play. Shocked, Neil's dad pulls him out of school to enroll him in military school. The boy commits suicide (offscreen) that night. Keating is blamed for the tragedy and gets fired. As Professor Keating collects his things from the classroom, the students rise on their desks and say to him, "O Captain, My Captain!"

    Dead Poets Society inspires young adults to follow their dreams and continues to resonate with viewers today. Watch the film, and then ask yourself: Was Keating a good professor?

Saw it! ☐ Rating: ☆☆☆☆☆

Date: ___/___/_____ With: _____

Notes: _____

_____

PRETTY IN PINK

THE STORY

Pretty in Pink stars Molly Ringwald as Andie Walsh in a role written specifically for her by John Hughes. Andie is a teenager who wears the wrong clothes, comes from a broken home, and works at the local mall—a combination that would certainly wreak havoc on any teenager's self-esteem. However, Andie is feisty and proud and won't conform to anyone's idea of what she should wear or who she should be. Moreover, she doesn't let the fact that she's poor get in the way of conquering her crush, Blane McDonnagh (Andrew McCarthy), a preppy boy at her school. He's a rich kid whose decision to become friends with Andie is questioned by his ultra-snobbish friend, Steff McKee (James Spader), who calls her "a mutant." Stuck in the "friend zone" is Duckie (Jon Cryer), Andie's good friend who constantly tries to get her attention with humor and clownish behavior.

DID YOU KNOW?

The ending of *Pretty in Pink* was reshot because teen test audiences didn't like that Andie ended up with Duckie in the original version.

WHY IT'S FAMOUS

This movie was written by John Hughes, who was considered the "teen-pic maestro" at the time with certified hits such as *Sixteen Candles* (1984) and *The Breakfast Club* (1985). The messages about Andie's security and self-confidence still inspire teenagers today.

DIRECTOR:
Howard Deutch

RELEASE DATE:
February 28, 1986

RATED:
PG-13
for adult situations/ language

RUNTIME:
1 hour, 36 minutes

Saw it! ☐ Rating: ☆☆☆☆☆

Date: ___/___/_____ With: _____

Notes: _____

_____

SCHOOL OF ROCK

DIRECTOR:
Richard Linklater

RELEASE DATE:
October 3, 2003

RATED:
PG-13
for some rude humor and drug references

RUNTIME:
1 hour,
48 minutes

THE STORY

Dewey Finn (Jack Black) is living out his dream of playing in a rock band. His dream is shattered when the guitarist takes a stage dive into the audience and the crowd doesn't even try to catch him. His band, No Vacancy, has also had enough of his over-the-top antics on stage and kicks him out of the band. Washed up and out of a job, the scruffy musician needs to pay his rent but hasn't had a gig for months. His roommate, Ned Schneebly, used to be in a band, but now has a regular job as a substitute teacher, and although he sympathizes with Dewey's situation, he gives him an ultimatum—pay the rent or move out. But rock 'n' roll is Dewey's life, and he doesn't know what else to do.

The phone rings with a call for Ned; the prestigious Horace Green prep school needs a substitute teacher. After hearing this, the proverbial light bulb clicks on in Dewey's head! He poses as Ned and takes the

job. However, instead of teaching the precocious fifth graders English or history, Dewey secretly instructs them on classic rock and how to play instruments so they can make their own band, complete with a manager, Summer Hathaway (Miranda Cosgrove), costume designer, and groupies. Obviously, this does not sit well with principal Rosalie "Roz" Mullins (Joan Cusack), who discovers Dewey's false identity and his plans to have the kids participate in a battle of the bands.

Meanwhile, Ned gets a check in the mail from Horace Green and discovers what Dewey has been up to. Dewey is trying to convince his buddy to not tell anybody about his impersonation scheme when Patty, Ned's girlfriend (Sarah Silverman), walks in on their conversation and hears about the elaborate deception. She calls the police, and Dewey's plan starts to fall apart. Or, does it?

WHY IT'S FAMOUS

School of Rock is a comedy with a serious undertone. The film's ability to reach both kids and adults with lessons about being passionate about something and pursuing it no matter what has made this a favorite family movie that's fun and entertaining to watch.

DID YOU KNOW?

Andrew Lloyd Webber (*Phantom of The Opera, Jesus Christ Superstar*) bought the rights to *School of Rock* and announced that a musical is in production.

STARRING:
Jack Black,
Miranda
Cosgrove,
Mike White, and
Joan Cusack

BOX OFFICE:
$131.2
Million

MUSIC:
Craig Wedren

Saw it! ☐ Rating: ☆☆☆☆☆
Date: ___/___/_____ With: _____
Notes: _____
_____

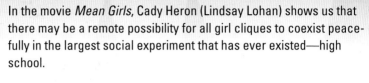

93

MEAN GIRLS

DIRECTOR:
Mark Waters

RELEASE DATE:
April 30, 2004

RATED:
PG-13
for sexual content, language, and some teen partying

RUNTIME:
1 hour, 37 minutes

In the movie *Mean Girls*, Cady Heron (Lindsay Lohan) shows us that there may be a remote possibility for all girl cliques to coexist peacefully in the largest social experiment that has ever existed—high school.

THE STORY

Cady moves to the suburbs from Africa, where she was home-schooled by her zoologist parents, and enrolls in Evanston Township High School in Illinois. She becomes friends with the goth-like Janis

(Lizzy Caplan) and Damian (Daniel Franzese), who is gay. They explain the social hierarchy on campus to Cady. The Plastics are the popular group and are led by Regina George (Rachel McAdams), Gretchen (Lacey Chabert), and Karen (Amanda Seyfried). One day, Regina eyes Cady and invites her to sit with her group at lunch. Janis jumps up and tells Cady to do it, thinking that she can spy on the Plastics and get some gossip that will bring down the vile girls' group once and for all. However, Cady has little experience navigating the treacherous high school social scene, and she thinks the Queen Bee actually likes her. Cady gradually changes her personality and adopts the Plastics' superficial and spiteful attitude. Things take a turn when Cady develops a crush on Regina's ex-boyfriend, Aaron Samuels (Jonathan Bennett), and the alpha girl gets jealous. To show her who's boss, Regina steals back her old boyfriend from Cady, humiliating her in the process. Things start to get ugly after Cady pulls a series of stunts to get revenge on Regina, essentially turning herself into the new Queen Bee. She causes a riot at school, but Ms. Norbury (Tina Fey), Cady's math teacher, hauls all of the girls into the gym and tries to make them understand that they are all at fault in creating this mess. Will Cady be able to turn things around?

STARRING:
Lindsay Lohan, Rachel McAdams, Lacey Chabert, Amanda Seyfried, and Tina Fey

BOX OFFICE:
$129 million

SCREEN-PLAY WRITTEN BY:
Tina Fey

DID YOU KNOW?

The script was written by Tina Fey (*Saturday Night Live, 30 Rock*), and based on the non-fiction book by author Rosalind Wiseman, *Queen Bees and Wannabes: Helping Your Daughter Survive Cliques, Gossip, Boyfriends, and Other Realities of Adolescence* (2002).

Saw it! ☐ Rating: ☆☆☆☆☆

Date: ___/___/_____ With: _____

Notes: _____

_____

94

FERRIS BUELLER'S DAY OFF

DIRECTOR:
John Hughes

RELEASE DATE:
June 11, 1986

RATED:
PG-13
for adult situations/ language

RUNTIME:
1 hour, 43 minutes

Who hasn't lied about having a stomachache to get out of going to school? Maybe you have a test you didn't study for or you didn't finish your homework. In *Ferris Bueller's Day Off*, Ferris Bueller (Matthew Broderick) decides to ditch school for an entirely different reason: "Life goes by so fast that if you don't stop and look around, you might miss it," he says.

THE STORY

Ferris is the typical popular high school slacker. Addressing the camera (which is called "breaking the fourth wall" in film speak), the high school senior narrates his bold day off. He convinces his girlfriend, Sloane Peterson (Mia Sara), and his gloomy best friend, Cameron (Alan Ruck), to join him. Bueller fast-talks Cameron into borrowing his dad's cherished 1961 fire-engine-red Ferrari 250 GT convertible, and they take it on an unforgettable joyride around Chicago.

They visit the Sears Tower (renamed the Willis Tower in 2009), gawk at masterpieces at the Art Institute, watch a Cubs game at Wrigley Field, and crash a parade float, where Bueller grabs the microphone and sings "Twist and Shout" with a marching band backing him up. They bamboozle their way into a fancy restaurant and have lunch. As they're leaving, they almost get caught by Ferris's father! Meanwhile, suspicions arise about Bueller's absence when his teacher (portrayed by Ben Stein) is taking attendance and repeats in a now-famous monotone voice, "Bueller? Bueller? Anyone, anyone?" The school principal, Edward Rooney (Jeffrey Jones), has had it with Bueller and his cocky attitude. Even Bueller's sister, Jeanie (Jennifer Grey), is mad that he's able to get away with everything. Rooney heads to the rogue teenager's home, determined to catch Bueller in the act and punish the trickster. The truant student's antics become more and more incredible as the infamous day off progresses. How will Ferris Bueller save the day—and his high school diploma?

FUN FACT
Ben Stein was a speech writer for former U. S. Presidents Richard Nixon and Gerald Ford.

STARRING:
Matthew Broderick, Mia Sara, Alan Ruck, Jeffrey Jones, and Jennifer Grey

BOX OFFICE:
$70.1 million

SCREEN-PLAY WRITTEN BY:
John Hughes

DID YOU KNOW?
John Hughes intentionally featured Chicago sites and landmarks as a tribute to the city where he grew up.

Saw it! ☐ Rating: ☆☆☆☆☆

Date: ___/___/_____ With: _____

Notes: _____

_____

95

SPELLBOUND

DIRECTOR:
Jeffrey Blitz

RELEASE DATE:
June 27, 2003

RATED:
G
General Audiences

RUNTIME:
1 hour,
37 minutes

Spellbound follows eight children between the ages of 10 and 14 as they prepare to compete in the 1999 Scripps National Spelling Bee held in Washington, D.C.

THE STORY

Nupur Lala comes from a family of Indian descent who believes that in America, if you work hard, you will succeed. Angela Arenivar is from a small town in Texas. She taught herself how to spell because her parents immigrated from Mexico and barely speak English. Ashley White lives in the housing projects in Washington, D.C. and gets help from her teachers. Neil Kadakia has a doting father

134

and professional coaches and courses to help him master his spelling skills.

April DeGideo's parents are also consumed with helping her study words. Ted Brigham is from Missouri, and his above-average intelligence makes him stand out. Emily Stagg is from a wealthy Connecticut family and studies spelling while also juggling riding and choir lessons. Harry Altman makes faces when trying to spell a word, and he tells jokes.

STARRING:
Angela Arenivar, Ubaldo Arenivar, and Jorge Arenivar

WHY IT'S FAMOUS

Imagine trying to learn all the words in a dictionary. That's what contestants have to do for the annual Scripps National Spelling Bee. The preparation, commitment, and willpower shown by the students in this documentary are simply amazing! Who wins this spelling bee? I can tell you this: After you watch *Spellbound*, the clear winner will be you!

BOX OFFICE:
$5.5 million

DID YOU KNOW?

Webster's Third New International Dictionary is the official dictionary of the Scripps National Spelling Bee. It has 476,000 word entries.

SCREEN-PLAY WRITTEN BY:
Jeffrey Blitz

Saw it! ☐ Rating: ☆☆☆☆☆

Date: ___/___/_____ With: _____

Notes: _____

_____

1 ACADEMY AWARD

96

MARCH OF THE PENGUINS

DIRECTOR:
Luc Jacquet

RELEASE DATE:
July 22, 2005

RATED:

G

General
Audiences

RUNTIME:
1 hour,
20 minutes

THE STORY

Imagine living in Antarctica. Sounds cold, right? To film *March of the Penguins*, a camera crew was stationed in the sub-zero climate for over a year! They documented the emperor penguin migration from the ocean to its arctic mating ground.

The footage captured during the months of filming in the harshest and coldest climate on earth (sometimes at -80 degrees!) reveals the struggles the emperor penguins endure to produce their young every year, including walking hundreds of miles to a particular area in the Antarctic where they settle to have their family. While the mothers go back to the ocean in search of food, the males sacrifice comfort, food, and experience loneliness to ensure their single egg safely hatches into a chick.

DID YOU KNOW?
Emperor penguins can grow to be 4 feet tall, and they can hold their breath underwater for up to 20 minutes.

WHY IT'S FAMOUS

March of the Penguins was a very successful film because it showed nature in its true habitat—not one fabricated in a movie studio or enhanced by special effects. Filming in an environment like the Antarctic hadn't been done like this before, and it presented a true test for the camera crew, who had to wear six layers of clothing to film for only three hours each day!

You'll also have newfound respect for these tall, flightless birds after watching this film. The next time you see emperor penguins at the local zoo, you'll understand that they are amazing creatures!

Saw it! ☐ Rating: ☆☆☆☆☆
Date: ___/___/_____ With: _____
Notes: _____
_____

SUPER SIZE ME

THE STORY

Morgan Spurlock decided to eat McDonald's for a month and make a documentary about the experiment. He graduated from New York University's film program in 1993, and he was inspired to make this movie by a news story about two teenage girls suing McDonald's for making them fat. Spurlock wanted to find out if this could really happen. He made some rules to follow from February 1 to March 2, 2003. He had to eat breakfast, lunch, and dinner only at McDonald's; supersize his meal when it was offered; and consume every item on the menu at least once during the 30 days.

Spurlock started his experiment weighing 185 pounds at 6'2" tall. He incorporated an average American's walking regimen of 5,000 steps, or 2 miles, per day. In this film you can see the physical transformation he undergoes after just 30 days of his "McDiet." His liver shows toxic signs equal to that of a binge-drinker and he develops heart palpitations, among other negative side effects. Throughout the documentary, he is supervised by a cardiologist, a gastroenterologist, and a general practitioner. He also has a nutritionist and a personal trainer.

How much weight did Spurlock gain, and how long did it take him to get back to his original self? Watch the film to find out.

DID YOU KNOW?

McDonald's phased out their Super Size program the same year this documentary was released.

DIRECTOR:
Morgan Spurlock

RELEASE DATE:
May 21, 2004 (Canada); June 11, 2004 (USA)

RATED:
PG-13
for thematic elements, a graphic medical procedure, and some language

RUNTIME:
1 hour, 40 minutes

Saw it! ☐ Rating: ☆☆☆☆☆
Date: ___/___/_____ With: _____
Notes: _____
_____

98

LINCOLN

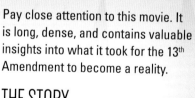

DIRECTOR:
Steven
Spielberg

**RELEASE
DATE:**
November 16, 2012

RATED:
PG-13
for an intense
scene of war
violence, some
images of carnage
and brief strong
language

RUNTIME:
2 hours,
30 minutes

Pay close attention to this movie. It is long, dense, and contains valuable insights into what it took for the 13th Amendment to become a reality.

THE STORY

In this political drama of epic proportions, we learn that Lincoln (portrayed by British actor Daniel Day-Lewis) was a humble man from even more humble origins. The movie begins in 1865 with Lincoln already in the White House dealing with the imminent end of the Civil War, but there's also a personal battle the president has been fighting. He's afraid the Emancipation Proclamation of 1863 will be repealed by the courts once the war is over. Lincoln

thought slavery was immoral and wanted to end it once and for all. To secure votes for the amendment, Lincoln uses lobbyists (John Hawkes, Tim Blake Nelson, and James Spader) to bribe and threaten reluctant Congressmen and offers federal jobs to outgoing Democratic congressmen. Adding to the problem are the Republicans who want an end to the Civil War sooner rather than later—something Lincoln knows will hinder the amendment's passing. Lincoln's political prowess comes into play, and we see how the 16th President of the United States keeps all factions at bay until the day of the crucial vote.

Meanwhile, Lincoln is also a husband and father. Mary Todd Lincoln (Sally Field) is not happy at the White House—the social demands are too much for her. She is also grieving the loss of one son, while coping with anxiety for her other son, Robert, who left college to serve in the war. How does the Lincoln family hold up during these difficult times?

As the film winds down, a relieved Lincoln is talking with his close advisers, when he is called away to join Mary at Ford's Theatre. "I suppose it's time to go, though I would rather stay," Lincoln says as he walks away.

STARRING:
Daniel Day-Lewis, Sally Field, David Strathairn, Tommy Lee Jones, and James Spader

BOX OFFICE:
$275.2 million

DID YOU KNOW?

DVDs of Steven Spielberg's *Lincoln* were donated to all middle schools and high schools, public or private, in the United States.

MUSIC:
John Williams

Saw it! ☐ Rating: ☆☆☆☆☆

Date: ___/___/_____ With: _____

Notes: _____

_____

99

APOLLO 13

DIRECTOR:
Ron Howard

RELEASE DATE:
June 30, 1995

RATED:
PG
for language and emotional intensity

RUNTIME:
2 hours,
20 minutes

THE STORY

Jim Lovell (Tom Hanks) wasn't supposed to be on Apollo 13, the third scheduled lunar landing of the NASA space program. Command unexpectedly informs him that he will lead the crew on this mission, instead of Apollo 14 as originally planned. The flight surgeon then tells Lovell that all three members of the crew have been exposed to the measles and that Ken Mattingly (Gary Sinise), who has not had the measles before, is at risk of getting sick during the mission.

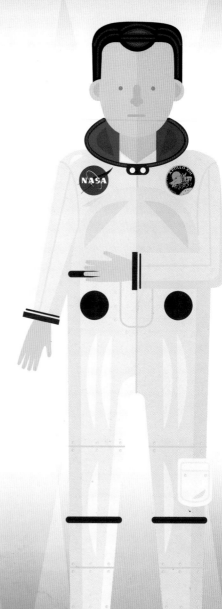

His substitute is Jack Swigert (Kevin Bacon), who joins Fred Haise (Bill Paxton) and Lovell on the crew.

Once in space, an air tank suddenly explodes and the astronauts' oxygen supply begins to vent into space. The blast also damages their electrical source, limiting their power capabilities and putting their ability to re-enter the Earth's atmosphere at risk. The three men seem doomed to either freeze to death or run out of oxygen unless they can repair the craft and steer it back home. Using everything on board, from a brush to a sock, the engineers fix one thing after another in a desperate race to get home. On the ground, Flight Director Gene Kranz (Ed Harris) instructs Mission Control to bring the astronauts home saying, "Failure is not option."

WHY IT'S FAMOUS

This film retells the true story about the ill-fated Apollo 13 lunar mission in 1970. Astronauts Jim Lovell, Fred Haise, and Jack Swigert made it back from outer space alive due to their bravery, ingenuity, and the incredibly bright team on the ground at NASA.

STARRING:
Tom Hanks,
Gary Sinise,
Bill Paxton,
Kevin Bacon,
and Ed Harris

BOX OFFICE:
$355.2 million

SCREEN-PLAY WRITTEN BY:
William Broyles Jr. and Al Reinert

DID YOU KNOW?

The famous quote, "Houston, we have a problem" is actually a misquote. The original line uttered by Jack Swigert was "Houston, we've had a problem here."

Saw it! ☐ Rating: ☆☆☆☆☆
Date: ___/___/_____ With: _____
Notes: _____
_____

PEARL HARBOR

DIRECTOR:
Michael Bay

RELEASE DATE:
May 25, 2001

RATED:
PG-13
for sustained intense war sequences, images of wounded, brief sensuality and some language

RUNTIME:
3 hours, 3 minutes

This fictional version of the attack on Pearl Harbor has plenty of explosions and graphic depictions of the horrors of war in order to give you a sense of what it was like to be in the middle of this infamous day in history.

THE STORY

Rafe McCawley (Ben Affleck) and Danny Walker (Josh Hartnett) are childhood friends living in Tennessee in 1923. They grow up and become lieutenants in the U.S. Army Air Corps, where Rafe meets Evelyn Johnson (Kate Beckinsale), a Navy nurse, and falls in love.

However, Rafe is committed to volunteering with the Royal Air Force and soon leaves for England, promising Evelyn he'll come back for her. Evelyn and Danny are transferred to Pearl Harbor, Hawaii. Reports say Rafe was shot down flying over the English Channel, and Danny and Evelyn bond over the loss of their friend. But Rafe didn't die, and when he comes back, he finds his friends are now a couple. Rafe and Danny get into a bar brawl and part ways that night. Little did they know that the next morning, December 7, 1941, they'd be attacked by Japanese bomber planes.

Danny and Rafe jump in their planes and mount a counter offensive against the Japanese. The raid sinks the USS *Arizona*, the USS *Oklahoma*, and several other ships. There are many casualties, and dozens of wounded fill the unprepared hospital. A few days later, both pilots are promoted to captain as the USA declares war on Japan. President Franklin D. Roosevelt (Jon Voight) orders a secret mission to bomb Japan. Danny and Rafe are assigned by Colonel Doolittle (Alec Baldwin) to bomb Tokyo and other Japanese towns. Before they leave, Evelyn tells Rafe a secret that he needs to keep from Danny—at least until they come back from the secret mission. Do they make it back? And what does Evelyn have to hide?

STARRING:
Ben Affleck,
Josh Hartnett,
Kate Beckinsale,
Jon Voight, and
Alec Baldwin

BOX OFFICE:
$449.2 million

DID YOU KNOW?

The Doolittle Raid of Tokyo took place in April of 1942 as retaliation for Pearl Harbor.

MUSIC:
Hans Zimmer

Saw it! ☐ Rating: ☆☆☆☆☆
Date: ___/___/_____ With: _____
Notes: _____
_____

101

HUGO

DIRECTOR:
Martin Scorsese

RELEASE DATE:
November 23, 2011

RATED:

PG

for mild thematic material, some action/peril, and smoking

RUNTIME:
2 hours, 6 minutes

THE STORY

Hugo Cabret (Asa Butterfield) learns to love films from his father, an inventor (Jude Law). Tragically, he becomes an orphan after his father dies in a fire. The only thing left from his father is a broken automaton—a robot—that should be able to write with a pen. Hugo now lives with his uncle in a secret room deep within a magnificent Parisian train station. He learns to fix clocks from his uncle, whose job is to wind and maintain the station's clocks every day. He's also determined to fix the automaton with help from his father's notebook and blueprints, because he's sure his father left a message for him to discover. To do this, Hugo steals toy parts from a bad-tempered store owner, Georges Méliès (Ben Kingsley). Méliès was once a famous French filmmaker, but Hugo is unaware of the grumpy man's past. One day, Méliès catches Hugo stealing a small toy and snatches his notebook as punishment. Hugo follows Méliès home, hoping to take back his notes. When the man leaves, Hugo sneaks in and encounters Isabelle (Chloë Grace Moretz), Méliès's goddaughter. She loves books and saves Hugo's notebook. They become friends and sneak into movies together. Surprisingly, they discover that Méliès was once a highly regarded actor as well. The kids decide to help the once-great cinema star realize that his films are still admired. Will Hugo fix the robot and find out if it has a secret message for him?

This is Martin Scorsese's first family film, and the first time the legendary storyteller used 3-D cameras.

Saw it! ☐ Rating: ☆☆☆☆☆

Date: ___/___/_____ With: _____

Notes: _____

_____